A notable cont ... his is a refreshingly access ...

... , Acts 29

Whilst the recent upsurge in church planting is hugely encouraging, church revitalisation has all too often been neglected as a vital strategy for re-evangelising the nation. In this new book John James makes a compelling case for the importance of church revitalisation. Written with a pastor's heart, and drawing on his experience as a practitioner at Crossways Church in Birmingham, he explains the theological foundations for revitalising churches, presents an inspiring vision of the gospel potential of revitalisation and shares practical wisdom for those leading church revitalisations. Written in a lively, accessible and engaging style, and drawing on case studies of successful church transformations from across the country, this book will challenge present and future church leaders to reconsider their attitudes towards declining and dying churches. I hope this book is a great success – it deserves to be. I look forward to promoting it.

John Stevens – National Director, FIEC

John James' book is a passionate call to consider the option of church revitalisation as part of our evangelism strategy. It is grounded in life experience but it contains much more than the story of a church that was close to death and then experienced new life. Running through this book is a heart for the lost, a desire to reach out to our marginalised communities and a commitment to work hard in tough, unglamorous settings. John's book is full of practical, hard-learned lessons which have application far beyond the situation he is describing. Much of this was directly relevant to my own situation, church planting in Lancaster. At every point he directs our gaze at God, his word, his work and his strength. I thoroughly recommend anyone considering pioneering a new work to read this book.

Karen Soole – Chair of the Northern Women's Convention

John captures both the joys and pain of taking a church from sickness to health. This book, born out of a personal faith in what God can do, will inspire and encourage you to see revitalisation as a God-given opportunity for the spread of the gospel in the UK. John is to be commended for his honest appraisal.

Phil Walter – Church Revitalisation Coordinator, FIEC

This book is a passionate plea for more people to engage in the demanding but joyful adventure that is church revitalisation. It is filled with honest reflections, heart-warming examples and God-glorifying hope. It offers a compelling case for why revitalisation is vital if we are to see gospel churches existing in the maximum number of places. There is so much wisdom in this book. I now have a long list of precious truths that will help us reach out more effectively as a local church.

Lee McMunn – Associate Minister, Riverside Church, Hull

RENEWAL

RENEWAL

CHURCH REVITALISATION ALONG THE WAY OF THE CROSS

JOHN JAMES

10 Publishing
a division of 10 of those.com

First published in Great Britain in 2016

British Library Cataloguing in Publication Data

A record for this book is available from the British Library

ISBN: 978-1-911272-07-6

Designed and typeset by Pete Barnsley (Creative Hoot)

Printed in the UK by CPI

10Publishing, a division of 10ofthose.com
Unit C, Tomlinson Road, Leyland, PR25 2DY, England

Email: info@10ofthose.com
Website: www.10ofthose.com

CONTENTS

FOREWORD

I am a fan, advocate and practitioner of church planting. I have given most of my life to the pursuit of church planting. I lead Acts 29, which is a *'diverse, global family of church planting churches'*. I am a passionate advocate of identifying Gospel Priority Areas – places and people where Christ is neither named nor known so that churches can be planted there. Which is why I am honoured to write a foreword to a book on church revitalisation!

There is a rich theological connection between planting and revitalisation, namely the doctrine of the church. Both are necessary theological endeavours because of the central place the church occupies in the kingdom of God.

Now of course, there is a difference between the two. In the sense described within this book, church revitalisation projects, like the type described here, are not referenced in the New Testament. Those churches among the seven in Asia Minor facing the prospect of candlestick removal were not presented as ripe for a new team to go in to turn them around. Church planting, however, is continually referenced as the way that the apostles obeyed the Great Commission.

But in post-Christian contexts like the UK and Europe, church revitalisation is a pressing need to be met and a gospel opportunity to be exploited. John James makes the case for it so well in this short and refreshingly accessible book. He writes with conviction. John is no easy pragmatist. He works hard at applying biblical principles to the task in hand. He also writes as a practitioner. But there is not a hint of the arrogance of '*been there, done that, got the scars*' attitude, to which practitioners can be so easily prone. He writes as someone who loves Jesus, the church and people. In putting the book together, he also had the nous to utilise the experience of others. The sections where he draws on the wisdom of Steve Robinson, Tim Sunderland, Peter Walkingshaw, Phil Walter and Duncan Woods should not be seen as mere fillers. There is much to be gleaned from their gospel ambition.

I was once in a lunch meeting, hosted by some Americans. I declined the offer of a cup of tea for the simple reason that my experience of tea made by Americans is not altogether positive. However, when I looked at the tea others had handed to them, I changed my mind and requested a cup. I'm glad I did. It was an excellent cuppa! I expressed my appreciation, and as a tea-loving Englishman, that commendation carried considerable weight with my hosts.

So it is with this commendation. For all my 'credentials' as a church planter, The Crowded House in Sheffield is actually a revitalisation project. Over a decade ago, I took a group of 20 to join an ageing and dwindling congregation. We are now significantly larger and have the privilege of being involved in gospel expansion not only around our city but into the world. This means I know a thing or two about revitalisation. So when I say I not only enjoyed this book but learned from it, shouldn't that carry some weight?

This is a good book. In many ways it's a primer, but that doesn't make it any the less important or significant. It's addressing an important and pressing issue. John has made a notable contribution to a great gospel cause.

Steve Timmis,
Executive Director, Acts 29

ACKNOWLEDGEMENTS

I am grateful to Steve Robinson, Tim Sunderland, Peter Walkingshaw, Phil Walter and Duncan Woods for providing such honest and thoughtful case studies for the book. Much thanks goes to Phil Topham, Jonathan Carswell and Lois Ferguson for encouraging the book to be written. I also am indebted to Ralph Cunnington and David Shaw for their advice and suggestions. We should all be grateful to Sam Parkinson for his careful editing, turning a convoluted stream of consciousness into slightly more precise prose. There are too many people to thank in relation to the last five years this book chronicles, but I hope what follows makes it clear that my dear brothers and sisters at Crossway Church are the real servant-hearted heroes of our tale. And, even though it is probably the last thing she would ever want to read, this is for Sarah, my wife, and dearest friend.

INTRODUCTION

At the front of our church building, by the pavement, is a flowerbed. I can call it a flowerbed now, but when we arrived it grew only brambles. It was a bramble-bed. Occasionally, during a tidy-up day the thorns would be hacked back in order to avoid a public health emergency. The soil was thin, dusty and anaemic. And it was at the bottom of my list of priorities.

By the grace of God, a few years ago, we had the privilege of baptising a retired couple with green fingers. They quietly began to take responsibility for the grounds around our building. Our crisis management was replaced by their careful nurture. With triffids uprooted, branches pruned, loam worked and blades clipped, the hostile horticulture was led into flourishing new life.

I had written off the bed, but they got to work. They cleared the brambles, digging up the whole root system. They added organic matter to the dusty soil. They discovered hidden plants that were being choked. They planted beautiful flowers. They laboured tirelessly, patiently, and consistently. The result is incredible.

A few weeks ago we conducted the first wedding in our building for many years. A young local couple with school-age children both became Christians. They were now taking an important step of obedience, honouring God in their relationship. Marvelling at the way Jesus had transformed this family, I glanced at the flowerbed. This is what God does. He works tirelessly, patiently, and consistently in our lives: digging up weeds, enriching soil, sowing the seed of his word, and growing us into the likeness of his Son. He delights to do it with us, and with his church. It is painful and messy, but it is real and glorious.

Crossway Church in Northfield, Birmingham is one of God's flowerbeds. He has tended it since 1937, but in 2009 it was looking dilapidated. There were around 14 active members left, and the one remaining elder was prayerfully considering how to wind things down over the next two years. I had preached there a handful of times, but my wife, Sarah, knew the church well. She had attended the Sunday school, and her parents were still members.

We were entering our final year at theological college, had a passion for the city of Birmingham, and for church planting. But we couldn't help thinking about Helier Chapel, as it was then known. The church family had a clear love for Jesus, his word, and their community. The context was strategic, with a great building in the heart of a needy community. At the time there was no other obvious gospel witness in the area. So the conversations began, and the church called us to a work of revitalisation. We arrived in September 2010 with a small core team of eight to get started.

No one is more surprised than me that this book has come out of that. It began as a series of short reflections, designed for a website, that quickly got out of hand. It isn't intended to be an authoritative manifesto or definitive how-to manual. But I have tried to write a book I would have appreciated back in 2010 as we set out on our journey. It is not an argument for a particular church polity, leadership style, theological vision or missiological approach. However, I hope it will be obvious that certain convictions about church, leadership, theology and mission underpin the approach we have taken. I have drawn heavily on the story of Crossway Church, but a number of case studies from other churches provide a wider perspective.

The purpose of the book is simple:

> *To make the case for revitalisation as a God-honouring, achievable and strategic means of church planting that has a vital role to play in the re-evangelisation of our nation.*

This is my conviction, and what we have found. My prayer is that this slim volume will be a blessing to those who read it. May it envision struggling churches wondering what the future holds. May it encourage larger churches uncertain of the strategic benefits of partnership with struggling churches. May it challenge individuals considering embarking on this journey. May it instruct leadership teams beginning those first tentative steps of change. May it bless you, wherever you are on this journey.

CHAPTER 1:

THE WAKE-UP CALL

'In our culture Christianity is a bit like a bad dream, the details of which you cannot quite remember, but which has left you with a sense of unease that you want to be rid of.'[1]

The spiritual climate in the UK was recently brought home starkly to me. I received a phone call from an Iranian lady who got my number from the church notice board. She had been reading the New Testament, had become convinced that Jesus was God, and wanted someone to confirm her suspicions for her. We talked together at length and her grasp of the gospel was breath-taking. All I did was show her, from the Scriptures she had already read, the truth of the conclusions she had already reached. It was an immense privilege.

I put down the phone, and went to see a young couple who had asked for a visit. They are born-and-bred Brummies, living on our estate, just a few doors down from our church building. They talked about a very serious life event they had been going through, and I began to tell them about Jesus. It was clear that they had never heard the gospel before. I shared the good news as best I could, and they both sat on the edge of the sofa, hanging on every word, jaws literally dropping.

It was a good day to be a church pastor, but it was also a wake-up call. This young couple had lived their whole lives in a supposedly 'Christian country' but had only ever heard the name of Jesus as a swearword, whilst the Iranian lady had grown up in an Islamic republic but had grasped the central aim of the gospel writers more deeply than some preachers I have heard.

Writing about the religiously unaffiliated in the United States, James Emery White speaks of a 'seismic shift in outreach that few church leaders are understanding.'[2] Evangelist Rico Tice detects a similar earthquake that has taken place in the UK over the last 70 years.

He explains that in 1954 Billy Graham packed out stadiums night after night. He preached the gospel and many became Christians because the basics were already in place. By 1994 there were barriers. Christianity was 'weird, untrue and irrelevant', and longer evangelistic courses like Alpha or Christianity Explored were needed to give the gospel a hearing. But today, 'we're such a long way from biblical Christianity that people don't object to faith having engaged with it; they simply dismiss it. Jesus simply isn't on the agenda; he isn't even an option to be considered.'[3] Our culture has changed. It is time we got real.

Our inability to wake up and smell the coffee is having an inevitable impact on the church. According to Al Mohler, in the US 4,000 congregations close their doors every year, while only 1,000 evangelical churches are planted.[4] That may sound terminal, but Mohler uses the UK as a warning of the future. I am not sure this is an area in which we should be proud of leading the way. Between 2008 and 2013, 2,071 churches closed in the UK. In that same period 1,224 were planted.[5] The alarm should be ringing. However, desperate to remain positive, we keep on hitting the snooze button.

First, in order to avoid the wake-up call, we find ways to inflate or hype church planting statistics. Church planting is vital and encouraging, but it can also be over-reported. I have noticed for example, that sometimes 'Fresh Expressions', the Church of England and Methodist initiative that encourages new ways of being church, is included wholesale in the statistics. When the 1,780 Fresh Expressions congregations are added to the church planting figure, it gives a perception of overall growth. Fresh Expressions is a creative initiative helping many face seriously the challenges of reaching our culture with the gospel, but simply adding the figures to the church planting statistics is unhelpful. 75% of Fresh Expressions groups are messy church groups. Almost half Fresh Expressions groups meet once a month, and half meet during the week. Most are not newly established, independent congregations, but part of the outreach of existing churches.

Secondly, in order to avoid the wake-up call, we fail to properly acknowledge where much of the growth is coming from. For example, a large number of migrant Christians have moved into the UK, joined or planted churches. They are doing an important job of slowing decline and strengthening witness. It is wonderful to see such ethnically diverse congregations emerge, but let us not pretend that this is growth because we have woken up to the reality of our cultural situation. It is usually not growth through conversion, but growth through a kind of global church transfer.

As with all statistical analysis, it all depends on how you tell the story. There are some who are surprisingly buoyant about current trends, and it is possible that we have turned a corner. Though in a measured manner, Bob Jackson, writing concerning the Church of England, concludes that there is 'probable growth' and 'brighter prospects'. [6]

However, as I write today, another article has been published in a national magazine, chronicling the fading impact of Christianity in Britain.[7] As evangelicals, we assume that we must be the bit that is growing, and that the rest is in decline. We talk about how liberal and mixed denominations are in freefall, but between 2008 and 2013 many evangelical denominations experienced a net loss of churches.[8] Although some denominations have experienced growth, their increases in numbers of churches are very small.[9]

Within my own church family, the Fellowship of Independent Evangelical Churches, we have experienced modest growth. There is a real desire to church plant. Yet a lot of the recent growth has been because existing churches have chosen to join the fellowship. The numbers themselves also fail to report life on the ground. Within the FIEC, as of 2013, 44% of churches had a membership of 25 or less. It is not a crime to be a small church – but, strikingly, since 2006, 75% of those churches have been static or in decline. For churches with a membership of 10-19, 82% have been static or in decline. For churches with a membership of under ten, that figure rises to 98%.[10]

The statistics suggest that many churches struggle to be effective in evangelism and discipleship. Or course this is not a problem that is unique to small churches. More important than your present size is the story of how you got to where you are. Many of our churches talk about struggling to reach their community with the gospel, of managing plateau and decline, even when they look strong numerically.

I recently bought a new alarm clock. It is the most basic model that Wilko's sells. It cost £2, and does not look pretty. It is not digital, it does not light up in the dark, does not have a radio or make me a cup of tea. I got it because it does not have a snooze button. When the alarm goes off, snooze is not an option, and it is time to wake up.

As churches we are very good at hitting snooze, of telling the story in a way that gives us a little more sleep, a little more slumber, a little more folding of the hands. But now is the time to wake up. Early on in our church revitalisation, I sat down with an elderly gentleman who had resisted the proposed changes from the beginning. I asked him why he thought the church was at the point of closure. He replied, 'It just is. Churches are planted, they grow, they shrink, and then they die.'

He had not engaged the real problem – the struggle to reach our communities for Jesus. This is not business as usual. Over the next decade or two these churches will close and their buildings will be sold on. The small flicker of witness will be snuffed out; the ground will lay fallow once more. Al Mohler, addressing the Southern Baptists, urges them to become 'Generation Replant'.[11] We need to hear that call, recognising the unique window of opportunity we have in this generation.

If the statistics are right, then many churches are approaching an event horizon, a point of no return. The gravitational pull towards closure will soon become so great it will make escape impossible. Like a canoeist approaching the edge of the Niagara Falls, there is a clear window of opportunity where an about-turn can take place. But, if they are left to drift sleepily, it is only a matter of time before the current is too strong, and these declining churches will have closed their doors for good because no one sounded the alarm.

What Is Church Revitalisation?

As gospel-hearted people, who believe in the local church, there are many ways we must wake up to the cultural challenges around us. We need to plant new churches, raise up new leaders, learn how to evangelise confidently and effectively, pray, disciple, and train. Amongst all of that, the challenge of this book is that we wake up to the unique opportunities of a work that we easily overlook: church revitalisation.

> *Church revitalisation is a local church intentionally recovering its calling to make disciples of Jesus. It is a process of deliberate change in order to bring about a new beginning, with the goal of recovering a gospel frontier for mission, and re-establishing gospel growth within a church community.*

Healthy church revitalisation has five important characteristics:

1. Healthy Church Revitalisation Seeks to Reach Lost People

The goal in church revitalisation is very similar to that of church planting: a freshly established gospel witness within a community. The goal is not saving face, retaining a building, maintaining the programmes of the church, and postponing the inevitable. It is driven by a desire to honour God, take seriously Jesus' call to make disciples of all nations, and play a small but vital role in the re-evangelisation of our nation.

When Jesus entered Jerusalem he wept over the city unwilling to recognise God's King, saying, 'If you, even you, had only known on this day what would bring you peace' (Lk. 19:42). When was the last time we thought about our communities in those terms? 'Britain, if you only knew Jesus, who brings true peace!' Healthy church revitalisation is driven by broken-heartedness for lost people.

2. Healthy Church Revitalisation Recognises the Need to Change

For healthy church revitalisation to take place, a degree of self-awareness is required. The church family must admit together the reality of their situation, take ownership of the current decline, and intentionally seek change for the sake of the gospel. Not everyone will understand the problem, but amongst the leadership and key members revitalisation requires a conscious humbling, creating openness, allowing for help and real change.

Speaking to Christians scattered among the nations, James writes, 'Humble yourselves before the Lord, and he will lift you up' (Jas. 4:10). Whilst we are busy arguing amongst ourselves about who is the greatest, and who will sit at the right hand of Jesus in glory, he is calling us to deny ourselves, take up our cross, and follow him. Revitalisation is not about self-preservation, but self-sacrifice.

3. Healthy Church Revitalisation Produces Healthy Churches

This may seem obvious, but church revitalisation is not something different to local church ministry. Church revitalisation is not needed because 'church doesn't work anymore'. Though there may be many reasons why a church is dying, it cannot be because the biblical marks of a church are no longer relevant. The most important question we can ask is: where has healthy local church ministry been lost, and where does it need to be recovered?

The Pastoral Epistles are packed full of the characteristics of healthy local church ministry. In his final charge to Timothy, Paul writes, 'preach the word; be prepared in season and out of season; correct, rebuke and encourage – with great patience and careful instruction' (2 Tim. 4:2). Healthy church revitalisation listens to and submits to God's word, patiently and carefully, letting it form us as a family.

4. Healthy Church Revitalisation is Tailored to its Context and People

Church revitalisation takes many forms. It might look like a small core team of believers being planted into an already existing congregation and the appointment of a new pastor. It might require the complete closure and re-launch of a church. It might be a much slower transition, with the implementation of new leadership with fresh vision. It may be abrupt, with a church intentionally dying, in order to generously leave its facilities for a new church plant to use.

The decision of where a particular revitalisation sits on the spectrum is not a purely pragmatic one. It should be driven by love. It is a love for God that will drive us to make brave, faith-fuelled decisions. It is a love for unbelievers that will drive us to be as radical as is needed in the changes that take place. It is a love for our brothers and sisters in the existing church that will drive us to act with patience, gentleness and compassion. All three dimensions of love will result in a unique process that fits its context and its people.

5. Healthy Church Revitalisation Partners with Others

It would be easy to suggest that the key to revitalisation is a particular methodology, particular theological emphasis, or a particular charismatic personality. In actual fact, for most healthy church revitalisations it is particular *relationships* that make all the difference. Relationships will be developed between a new core team and an existing church family, between new and old leadership teams, and between the church undergoing revitalisation and other local gospel-hearted churches. Coming into a context of revitalisation there are pre-existing relationships that need to be understood and honoured rightly, and there will be crucial new relationships that will need to be forged for the work to flourish.

Paul prays at the end of Romans, 'May the God who gives endurance and encouragement give you the same attitude of mind toward each other that Christ Jesus had, so that with one mind and one voice you may glorify the God and Father of our Lord Jesus Christ' (Rom. 15:5–6). With that kind of generosity of spirit towards one another, anything is possible.

Putting it into Practice

A short while ago we marked a milestone as a church: we removed the old preacher's platform from our building. The wooden stage dated back to 1937 when the hall was built, and was later extended. It was high and hefty, and ripping it out took serious brute strength. Surely a book on revitalisation begins with conversions, baptisms and the reviving power of the Spirit of God? The preacher's platform was none of these things. It was a piece of furniture. Ripping out platforms is irrelevant to church revitalisation.

Except that, we removed the platform because it took up about one-eighth of the room, and we needed the space. Three people gave up two days, gaining many aching muscles, and grappling with nails and floorboards. Two of the three had stood on that platform, given their testimonies, and been baptised within the last three years. It was about reaching lost people.

Removing the platform was symbolic of a shift in priorities, as we were formed together as a family through the word of God. The fabric of our building is now of lower importance than making room for new people. It is about healthy church.

The platform was not ripped out for the sake of it, or because we had heard that another church had done something similar. It was the obvious next relevant thing that needed to happen, in our very specific journey as a church family. It is about our context.

And the removal of the platform, though unthinkable five years ago, was opposed by no one when it happened. We had built real trust. It was about relationships.

It is also worth stating one thing that healthy church revitalisation is *not*. It is not a covert strategy for asset stripping vulnerable churches. Hopefully, the five points above make clear that healthy revitalisation is driven by a love for God, his people, and the lost. As a pastor, the term 'revitalisation' carries no meaning if I have no intention of taking with me as many of the existing church family as is possible. Being driven by love in this way, in a specific context, is of course nothing very special and unique. Interestingly, Mark Dever, in interview, wondered if 'the language of revitalisation means anything different from what we call pastoring'.[12] Every church ought to maintain a posture of revitalisation, as it repents, believes, mortifies, and walks in obedience to the call of Christ.

It may be that for that reason church revitalisation as a 'thing' was not really spoken about much even five years ago. When we embarked on our project we were not even sure what to call what we were doing. At the time I could only find one popular-level book on the subject.[13] The recent interest in revitalisation, and the way that it has been linked to church planting, is very helpful. It takes seriously the cultural shift we have witnessed, recognises the danger of being unresponsive, and is perhaps a sign that we are, at last, beginning to wake up.

CASE STUDY 1:

REVITALISATION AND GOSPEL MULTIPLICATION

PETER WALKINGSHAW, CARLISLE BAPTIST CHURCH

My wife, Lucy, and I are both Cumbrians but had for some years lived outside the county. In 2009 we became aware that the congregation at Carlisle Baptist Church had declined to just a small number of mostly older believers, and that some folk were starting to consider closing the church. I approached the church and discussed with the leaders the possibility of coming to try and bring about a 'fresh start'.

After over a year of planning, Lucy and I moved to Carlisle with our family. We didn't bring a team from our existing church as we had moved from about three hours' drive away. The church had not had a pastor for a number of years and we had to hit the ground running from the first Sunday in September 2010, assessing where the church was at, and carefully attempting to build on the strengths and address some of the weaknesses.

We found that while there was a willingness in the congregation to reach out to non-Christians in our city, that task had become increasingly difficult as the congregation aged and reduced in number. In any age or situation, the church needs 'timeless truth matched with timely methods', and in our context, while the church was seeking to guard the timeless truth, it was struggling to present that in a way that connected with, and had meaning for, unchurched folk in Carlisle.

As we embarked on the process of revitalisation, a number of factors have contributed to it beginning to flourish. Of course it was God at work, but thinking practically, we had a lot of external prayer and financial support without which the changes would have been difficult. However, the bottom line is that it has been the willingness from the older folk to 'give new things a go' that really made progress possible.

In terms of my priorities, I knew that, then as now, the core of what we did had to be about our main Sunday morning meeting, and especially hearing God's word read and explained. All the other activities of the church flow from that. We also had to look at what we did, how we presented ourselves and spoke to people not familiar with church: from our website, to the language we used in our gatherings, to the focus of our prayer life. We had to consider what we could do to make it easier for new folk to come, and be engaged with the good news of Jesus.

As we have walked through this process, there are many encouragements I could speak of. One of the older folk told me that we had more baptisms in the church in the first two years from the 'fresh start' than in the previous 40 years of the church's history, and it has to be the folk coming to faith, and existing Christians being 're-energised' in their faith that has encouraged us most.

It has also been wonderful to see God use this process to then go on and multiply ministry around Carlisle. About three years after the 'fresh start' at Carlisle Baptist we had an approach from the leaders at a small church in the town of Brampton nine miles east of Carlisle. The largely elderly congregation had seen what had happened at our church and enquired about the possibility of us offering them some help. It was not immediately clear how we could help. But we began what turned out to be an 18-month process of prayer, fundraising and then finding and appointing a man to come and pastor that church.

As we prayed and worked through this process, four families with young children, who were part of our church but lived closer to Brampton carefully considered if they could move to support a fresh start at this other church. Wonderfully, all four families did decide to join the new pastor as he arrived, and that has given a great boost to this renewal work.

Of course, the revitalisation has also been hard at times. One of the biggest challenges in any church leadership is knowing that what is best for the church may not be best for every individual in the church, or at the very least, they may not *think* that it is best for them. Leading through that kind of situation can be tough.

I am a big fan of church planting, and I strongly believe that we need to plant brand new churches throughout the UK. However, I also strongly feel that some men who are drawn to planting have the grace, patience and endurance to go beyond simply starting afresh somewhere, and instead be used by God to bring new life to a dying congregation. If we are going to reach our nation for Christ, we need a lot more of both.

CHAPTER 2:

WHERE ARE WE GOING?

'Let no man who looks for ease of mind and seeks the quietude of life enter the ministry; if he does so he will flee from it in disgust.'[1]

At theological college the idea that moving to a dying church was something we might actually be considering was met predominantly with stunned silence or serious words of caution. Amongst the church family, though most were willing to try anything, there were a few who were actively against the proposal from day one. For my wife and I, when we paused for thought, it was hard to know if what we were preparing to embark on was an act of faithfulness or of foolishness.

It may be that we know of nightmare experiences of church revitalisation. The last thing I want to do is foster a naïve optimism that gently ushers ministerial lambs into the ecclesiastical slaughterhouse. To be fair, most churches would be horrified at the thought that they may be about to unintentionally chew up and spit out someone who has been recognised for pastoral ministry. There are also many horror stories of churches that placed unquestioning trust in a person, or a process, that lacked wisdom and badly damaged the church.

Some of the notes of caution about church revitalisation are valid, and my prayer is that the rest of this book will help you think through the process, and evaluate your own context with care. However, there are a number of common arguments against revitalisation that are, in the final analysis, nothing more than an unhelpful cultural bias under the guise of a concern for the local church. There are good reasons, and there are bad reasons, to be wary. I want to briefly look at three common pushbacks that may not be quite what they seem.

1. 'It Is Easier to Give Birth Than Raise the Dead.'

This is a pithy little phrase that was used more than once when we began to talk about revitalisation. It makes perfect sense. Why would you attempt resurrection, when the option of simply birthing a new church plant is open to you? There is an obvious logic to it. The task of revitalisation is *both* the turning around of an existing church family, *and* the breaking of new ground as you reconnect with the community and re-establish a frontier for the gospel. That is clearly twice as much work and twice as difficult.

It is like the tourist stopping to ask directions to the train station. The local replies, 'Well, I wouldn't start from here.'

It is easy to compare the starting point of a church plant, with its fired-up core team and blank sheet of paper to a church revitalisation, with a tired, disillusioned family and outmoded traditions, and consider it a no-brainer. 'Well, I wouldn't start from here.' The two starting points are different. It is essential to be honest with yourself and anyone else involved about the journey ahead.

But what do we mean by 'easier'? It is tempting to assume that with a church plant the route forward it relatively clear. But, wherever one begins, we can never decide the route without the people. We may have very clear convictions about the destination, but the route must always meet others where they are waiting to be picked up. However like-minded a freshly formed core team may be, no one is starting where you are. Whatever your model of church, fantasy needs to quickly become reality for a true community to form.

Church planting is not easy. A 2007 study in the US reported that a third of church plants they surveyed failed within four years of being planted.[2] A more recent UK report suggested that it would be right to expect one in four to fail within two years.[3]

I regularly meet with other church planters across the city of Birmingham. We offer peer-to-peer support, identifying what we are learning, sharing our struggles and praying for each other. One friend, a year into a church plant in an adjacent community to Northfield recently reflected, 'The abstract plans I made for how things would look didn't survive the first people agreeing to join us and have been ripped up and rewritten any number of times since the first service. Planting involves loving and pastoring real people and real people don't fit our plans as neatly as we would like them to.'

Dietrich Bonhoeffer writes,

> *Innumerable times a whole Christian community has broken down because it had sprung from a wish dream.*

> *The serious Christian, set down for the first time in a Christian community, is likely to bring with him a very definite idea of what Christian life together should be and try to realise it. But God's grace speedily shatters such dreams. Just as surely God desires to lead us to a knowledge of genuine Christian fellowship, so surely must we be overwhelmed by a great general disillusionment with others, with Christians in general, and, if we are fortunate, with ourselves.*[4]

Though we must start with a clear vision for our church, real community begins with disillusionment, and disillusionment is not far away in either a church revitalisation or a church plant. Sooner or later we all have to learn to love people more than we love the route that we have planned, and wherever we start from, that is never easy.

The other main issue with this argument is that it unnecessarily polarises 'giving birth' and 'raising the dead'. There are occasions when the biblical picture concerning the church is one of giving birth. Paul writes to the Galatians,

> *My dear children, for whom I am again in the pains of childbirth until Christ is formed in you, how I wish I could be with you now and change my tone, because I am perplexed about you!*
>
> Galatians 4:19–20

Leaving aside the fact that Paul's labour sounds excruciating, not easy, that kind of image is complementary to, not antithetical to, another dominant image in the New Testament concerning discipleship and gospel ministry.

Jesus says,

> *The hour has come for the Son of Man to be glorified. Very truly I tell you, unless a grain of wheat falls to the ground and dies, it remains only a single seed. But if it dies, it produces many seeds. Anyone who loves their life will lose it, while anyone who hates their life in this world will keep it for eternal life. Whoever serves me must follow me; and where I am, my servant also will be. My Father will honour the one who serves me.*
>
> John 12:23–26

The glorification of Jesus is pictured as a seed dying, and in dying, producing many new vibrant living seeds. In John's Gospel, the hour of Jesus' glorification is very clearly the crucifixion. Jesus then immediately extends the metaphor of a kernel of wheat dying to speak of the discipleship of 'anyone'. Hate your life, deny yourself, lose your life for me and for the gospel (c.f. Mk. 8:34–35) and you will find new life, eternal life, *resurrection* life.

But notice that Jesus applies the picture further still, spelling out the key component of discipleship: 'whoever serves' (Jn. 12:26). Serving Jesus will look like a seed falling to the ground and dying, and in doing so will produce many seeds. Paul writes, 'For we who are alive are always being given over to death for Jesus' sake, so that his life may also be revealed in our mortal body. So then, death is at work in us but life is at work in you' (2 Cor. 4:11–12).

The problem with the argument that 'it is easier to give

birth than raise the dead' is not so much that it misunderstands church planting (though it does), or that it misunderstands church revitalisation (though it does), but that it misunderstands discipleship and gospel ministry. Any and all of our Christian service requires death and resurrection, which means no form is 'easier' than any other. All of it is impossible, except for the reality of a life-giving God who delights to resurrect the dead.

2. 'I Don't Want to Get Stuck in the Past.'

There is something important to hear here. For some people, the desire for the renewal of their church is nothing more than a desire to return to 'the way things used to be'. In their minds, there was a point, usually in the 1950s, when the church was close to revival, every hymn moved them to tears, the preaching had *real* passion, and they tasted fellowship akin to the early chapters of the book of Acts (minus Ananias and Sapphira, of course). The request for revitalisation is nothing more than a request for a ticket back to a time when parents really knew how to discipline their children, we used jumpers for goal posts, and no one ever had to lock their doors.

To understand this hunger for history it may help to reflect on one of the greatest British success stories of the last few years: *Downton Abbey*. It attracted more than 10 million viewers a week in the UK, and by the end of its run was watched by 120 million people in some 200 countries.[5] Why? The historian Dominic Sandbrook argues 'that the key to the country-house drama is the atmosphere of romantic melancholy that comes when we realise that the foundations are beginning to crumble'.[6] As we lose the past, our obsession with the past only grows. Faced with

"RENEWAL"

1. Healthy Church revitalisation seeks to reach lost people.

2. Healthy Church revitalisation recognises the need to change.

3. Healthy Church revitalisation produces healthy churches.

4. Healthy Church revitalisation is tailored to its context and people.

5. Healthy Church revitalisation partners with others.

enormous cultural change, we try to escape into a paradise now lost beyond our grasp.

But, what paradise? As Sandbrook reflects, 'The early twentieth-century country house was built on deference, fear and backbreaking toil. Most servants worked for long hours in dreadful conditions … And far from becoming fast friends with their servants, many aristocrats barely recognised them as fellow human beings.'[7] None of this is acknowledged as we enter the TV world of the saintly and paternalistic Earl of Grantham. *Downton Abbey* is pure nostalgia, and nostalgia is *fiction*.

When this is translated into the context of church, it is no wonder that the pushback is automatically, 'I don't want to get stuck in the past.' The call to revitalisation is not a call to take part in a deluded period drama. In the face of the tide of change that we outlined earlier, the overwhelming urge to escape into a mythical golden age must be resisted at all costs. The past cannot change the present, outmoded models of ministry are precisely that – outmoded. Nostalgia breeds inertia. It makes us deaf to the alarm bell that must be allowed to rouse us from our slumber.

However, that we belong to a church that *has* a past is not in itself a bad thing. The 'past' is not a dirty word. Jesus says to the church in Ephesus, 'you have forsaken the love you had at first. Consider how far you have fallen! Repent and do the things you did at first' (Rev. 2:4–5). For the church in Ephesus it is their past faithfulness that is commended, and they must return to it. In that sense, the revitalisation of Ephesus comes not with a warning about becoming stuck in the past, but with a command to recover it.

Obviously the 'past' that is being spoken of in these verses is a recent past, which has quickly been forgotten. It is not quite the hankering after a bygone age. But it does serve to emphasise the fact that *we* all have a past. Church planting sometimes promises the idea of a blank sheet of paper, and the creation of 'a church for people who don't do church', but church plants themselves are full of people with a past they bring with them. It does not take long before tradition develops.

One author makes this observation, 'In my conversations with church planters over the years, I have asked them about tradition. Without exception, these individuals have all affirmed that, within seven years of founding their churches, deep-seated traditions became the norm and had to be addressed. Therefore, if we are drawn to church planting rather than church revitalisation because we reject tradition, we will be leaving our churches about every four to seven years.'[8] It really does not take long before the past is in danger of getting us 'stuck'.

Rather than be embarrassed by the past, we need to learn how to honour the past rightly. We did not discover the good news of Jesus. It was passed on to us, bequeathed to us by our forbears. In the UK, fresh urban church plants that grow quickly often do so because young people who join them have been nurtured in 'historic' and intergenerational community churches elsewhere. The historic foundation may be hidden, but it exists and is something for which we should be extremely thankful.

We love to separate ourselves from the past. I suspect that is why we measure everything in decades. It allows me to watch a programme about the nineties, laugh at their shell suits and pop records, tut at their unenlightened worldview, without facing the fact that 'they' was, and is, 'me.' Yet it may actually be the case that the past has something to teach us. We are not the only generation that has ever sought to minister faithfully. In Titus chapter 2 Paul suggests that healthy gospel ministry should necessarily include discipleship across the generations, with the older teaching the younger.

The argument 'I don't want to get stuck in the past' misunderstands the problem. We all have an unavoidable past that is part of us. But the right concern about nostalgia is actually not a problem with the past at all. Nostalgia is not so much driven by a love of the way things were, as it is by a fear of the way things are today. Which means the argument also misunderstands the goal of church revitalisation. Church revitalisation is not about preserving a musty museum piece with no connection to reality. It is about regaining our confidence in the truth that the Jesus of history, the Jesus of our history, is the same Jesus who is seated on the throne today.

3. 'It is Not a Strategic Use of Resources.'

We rightly want to be strategic. As conscientious Christians we will be concerned not to waste the resources God has given us, to reach as many people as we can with the opportunities we have been given, and to avoid spending time on unfruitful endeavours. It may be that for you, reading this book is an attempt to discover whether church revitalisation is a strategy actually worth the effort.

Dying churches have problems, or they would not be dying. Imagine you move house, and begin to look for a local church to attend. You decide to give St Brunhild Welcome Hall a try, and discover a church family disconnected from the local community;

little, if any, evangelism; no coherent pathway for discipleship; a small, tired, elderly congregation; overdependence on outside support; a building in disrepair; eccentric corporate worship; dominant personalities; a loss of confidence in the Bible; ambiguous governance; resistance to change; and a collective resignation to inevitable death. There is no obvious plan in place, and you will be attending as an outsider. A little 'strategic' thinking should rightly give you cause for concern.

Or imagine you are the minister of a church that is slowly but steadily growing, and you get a call for help from the leadership team of Clifftop Christian Fellowship. You drive the 30 minutes out into the countryside, to witness a very small but passionate community, meeting in a beautifully kept building, in the middle of nowhere. Three-quarters of the church family live within the area, but the area is a hamlet of 25 homes, surrounded by fields of sheep, and beyond the cliff, the North Sea. Strategic thinking will need to govern the type of support you are willing to offer.

There are right ways to think strategically, but there are also wrong ways to think strategically. So often when that kind of language is used it is based more on the world's logic than God's. For example, 'more strategic' does not imply something will be 'easier'. We have already seen that all gospel ministry requires death and resurrection, and that which is impossible for us is made possible by God.

How is revitalisation less strategic than planting? The implication is that it is likely to be a slower or more expensive process. It is true that two years in, compared with any church plant, it may look like it is seriously lagging behind. It may have been two years of slow change, with very little to show for it. But, five years in, compared with many church plants, it may look stronger because the pre-existent congregation are still present, and many of the assets of the church are retained. Actually, in terms of cost, the burden of church planting carried by any single church may well be significantly reduced if a revitalisation model is employed. It is likely to require a smaller core team, with a smaller budget, from the outset. If the church owns a building then less money will be spent on renting, and less time and energy will be spent negotiating and setting up a shared space each week. The result of this is, God willing, more time on the frontline of gospel ministry.

I want to suggest that if a 'Hub Church' is committed to raising up leaders, planting churches, and reaching a whole town or city for Christ, it will almost certainly need to consider church revitalisation as part of its strategy. It may not be a strategic use of resources for building a church empire, but if we have a kingdom mindset, and gospel generosity, then one of the most strategic things we can do is partner with other churches to help dying churches to grow again.

In our context a *strategic* relationship was developed with a small dying congregation through the preaching group of a hub church in the city. The preaching group itself was an important way young gospel minsters were being trained and having their calling tested. That helped to identify the church, and to build the trust necessary for conversations to begin. A *strategic* relationship was also developed between three growing churches that were committed to planting churches in order to reach Birmingham. That developed into a coalition of churches, now called 2020 Birmingham. It offered support that contributed to making a church revitalisation viable. *Strategic* relationships also developed between a number of local churches and myself as the planter. These churches may not have been able to resource the entire project, but were willing to encourage members of their congregation to consider joining the core team, were willing to help in any way they could, and were willing to pick up the phone and offer me much-needed mentoring when required.

The result is that a new gospel witness has been established in a community that makes up an important part of the city we are all trying to reach. Arguably, it would have been a larger drain on resources, and required a longer time frame, if we had planted instead. I want to ask, if you are in a hub church and want to be truly strategic, how open are you to church revitalisation, if the opportunity comes your way?

Finally, I suspect that often when the strategy argument is used, behind it is an assumption that church revitalisation itself is pointless. The unique benefits of church planting are absent, and all that is left is the heartache and pain. When church revitalisation is simply labelled 'not strategic,' there is an obvious blindness to the peculiar blessings that this kind of a model unearths. In the next chapter I want to briefly identify some of the real strategic benefits to church revitalisation that I have seen in our context.

CHAPTER 3:

IS THE JOURNEY WORTH IT?

'The Americans have need of the telephone, but we do not. We have plenty of messenger boys.'[1]

It would be easy to look at the task of church revitalisation as simply a massive headache to be avoided at all costs. It requires an agenda of change from day one. There is no honeymoon, no blank slate, and everything you do feels like a compromise. The present can be demoralising and your vision of the future can look impossible to realise. It demands risk, tenacity, patience and prayer. Why bother?

Logically, the most 'strategic' thing to do is to turn off the life support machine and give birth elsewhere. Why waste your time with musty, old, decaying churches when you could be planting nice, shiny, latte-sipping, skinny-jean wearing, beard-toting church plants?

Over the last few years, I have wondered whether revitalisation is best defined as 'church planting without the benefits'! But this is to misunderstand the task. I hope I am beginning to make the case for revitalisation, not as a necessary evil, or a 'poor man's church plant', but as a unique opportunity that will, alongside other models of planting, contribute to the re-evangelisation of our nation.

In this chapter I want to suggest six key benefits of revitalisation I have witnessed, and show you its gospel logic. These benefits show that there will be places in which revitalisation is logically and strategically the best option.

1. Revitalisation Grows Us in Our Love of Jesus

When Jesus speaks to the church in Ephesus he says, 'You have persevered and have endured hardships for my name, and have not grown weary. Yet I hold this against you: you have forsaken the love you had at first' (Rev. 2:3–4). Here is a church that has sought to 'hang on in there' with the odds stacked against them. Unfortunately it has been at the expense of their love for Jesus.

It is not hard for members of dying churches to end up in that place. They have fought. They are battle-worn and weary. But worse, in the process they have become cynical, disillusioned and have lost their first love. This is serious because Jesus concludes by saying, 'To the one who is victorious, I will give the right to eat from the tree of life, which is in the paradise of God' (Rev. 2:7). These are not just dying churches, but disillusioned saints, and eternity is at stake.

Being led through a process of revitalisation can become an incredible opportunity for repentance and doing again the things that were done at first (Rev. 2:5). In our context it has been wonderful to see a process of personal spiritual revitalisation going on amongst many of the original church family. These are not people who would hop on a bus to seek out a gospel-centred church in the next town, but who have nevertheless undergone renewal because it is happening in their church, in their community.

There is something amiss if a church planting methodology is developed that either intentionally or unintentionally marginalises the discipleship of older Christians. If God will preserve us, we all need to be able to say with Paul, 'the time for my departure is near. I have fought the good fight, I have finished the race, I have kept the faith' (2 Tim. 4:6–7). That is not a solitary task. We all need to belong to a church family that will help us get there. The renewal of dying churches can be a tool by which God renews his people. If we believe in the perseverance of the saints, we should believe in the revitalisation of dying churches.

But revitalisation does not only renew older Christians. It drives us all to great reliance on God. It is one thing to look at a blank sheet and pray for God to work, it is another thing to look at a sheet with detailed, messy, archaic prose written all over it, and ask for the same outcome from God. It is truly thrilling to embark upon something that demonstrably requires the miraculous recreational power of Jesus Christ from day one. Revitalisation grows believers in their love of Jesus.

2. Revitalisation Builds On the Past

Earlier, I briefly mentioned that church revitalisation is not a disguised form of asset stripping. However, if asset stripping is the practice of removing the wealth of an organisation with no regard for its future, then for a church that has a building and a bank balance to die without a responsible plan for the future is just as bad. The true asset strippers are not churches that engage in revitalisation but churches that die quietly without releasing those assets for future generations of gospel ministry.

I appreciate that those are blunt words. But the truth is, if Helier Chapel had not been willing to allow this process of revitalisation to take place, then the wider church would have lost a building in a strategic location, 75 years of history with a community, and a decent sum of money in the bank. And Crossway Church (our new name), if it had been viable at all, would have begun in a very different way. It is only because of the conviction of a few gospel-hearted people to see those assets remain in the kingdom, that we are where we are today.

It is easy to overlook just how significant the practical benefits of church revitalisation can be. I have recently been in conversation with another church considering revitalisation. As I walked down the long residential street, to find the venue, I discovered a remarkable facility nestled between two long terraces, and no other gospel witness in view. I could almost smell the opportunity.

When our church was planted in 1937, the Sunday school superintendent would walk around the local streets carrying a large placard that said 'Sunday School This Way'. The children would run out of the houses, and form a line behind him, all the way back to the church! Can you imagine that as an evangelism strategy today? And yet, I meet people most weeks who remember attending that Sunday school (not in the thirties, but certainly the sixties and seventies), and even the 60-year-old bloke who cuts my hair used to go as a boy. Our evangelism strategy today can build on the ministry of faithful men and women of the past.

We are not the only generation that has ever sought to minister faithfully. No community in the UK is a gospel vacuum. And revitalisation builds on the past.

3. Revitalisation Establishes Intergenerational Church from Day One

If you had a vision of what you would want the demographic of your church plant to look like after five years, it would not be long before the word 'intergenerational' was employed. In fact, most church plants I know that have been going for a while, some nearly ten years, are actively praying for an older generation of believers to be a part of their congregation. It is understandable that church plants often have a younger average age than established churches. Younger people may be more willing to move churches and take on a new challenge, and may have less invested in the church they leave. Whatever the reasons, the longing for more mature believers, at a different stage of life, who can take on the role of mothers, fathers, grandmas and grandpas, is often a very healthy one, recognising the complexity of the pastoral care that is required and the kind of people who are actually able to share that load.

If you then spoke with any of the churches that have identified themselves as in need of revitalisation, and asked them what they would want the demographic of their church to look like in five years' time, the word 'intergenerational' may well be used, but for exactly the opposite reason. Anyone under 60 would be nice!

Now, it is hardly rocket science, but if you plant a group of young people into an already existing, older congregation, and a good number of those people begin to grow again in their love for Jesus, a new intergenerational church will have begun. When I look at the demographic of Crossway Church, we are honoured to have a significant number of older members who are in turn delighted to see younger folk belonging to the family. Now, before you envisage some kind of utopia, an intergenerational community has significant pressures, but these pressures are welcome because the reality is that we have had from day one what other church plants are praying for years after planting. Rather than asking the older generation to up sticks and come to us, we have instead come to them.

The impact of this is undeniable. We have three generations of the same family in regular attendance in the church, and on occasions two different families have had four generations all sat together in church. Some of those will be believers, some on the fringe of church, some young children. They all feel able to engage with the church community regardless of their age differences. As people have joined the church we have not exclusively reached 'younger' people. We have baptised a retired couple, and had a number of older folk come and join the church, even though in many other ways we show all the signs of a young chaotic church plant. The impact of that has been that as church family there are lines of pastoral support in place that draw upon the wisdom that comes only with time.

4. Revitalisation Empowers Forgotten Believers

I want to briefly tell you about one of our members. Many decades ago, he had a dramatic conversion whilst peeling potatoes in the back of the chip shop where he worked. He gave his life to Jesus, stopped drinking, stopped smoking, and stopped swearing. He walked into the church a few doors up from him, and was welcomed, loved and discipled. He is pretty straightforward. He is loyal to Jesus, and he is loyal to the church family he loves. Unfortunately, the formal church family meetings were very close to ending because old age and dwindling numbers meant they were no longer viable.

When we arrived, he was one of the first people I met. He was the doorman, shaking everyone by the hand, calling everyone 'Bab', and making sure we all had Bibles. Within a few weeks of preaching through Mark's Gospel, I realised that every time I preached the gospel, he was leaning forward, with his Bible open, and with tears running down his face. I thought it was just my poor exegesis, but at the end of the service he was the first to come up, shake my hand and tell me how good God is.

The embers that had grown cold quickly fanned into flames again, and within a matter of weeks he became one of our best evangelists. He still is. He knows everyone on the estate, and tells everyone about Jesus. He is the first at church on a Sunday morning to open up. He is still the doorman, and is hugely encouraged by the number of people he now gets to call 'Bab'.

I dug out an email I had sent to a friend. We were three months in, and resistance against a reformed understanding of the gospel was being strongly felt. One guy was threatening to leave the church (which he later did). That had unnerved the leadership team as a whole, and it took everything I had, in fact *more* than I had, just to stand up and preach each week. But, God had opened my eyes to this particular member, and I wrote, 'On Sunday I felt

God saying, "That is why you didn't plant a church down the road ... that is why you are here trying to do this thing ... because he, and others just like him need feeding. They are my sheep and have just as much right to be fed as anyone else. It is worth the hassle for them.'" Revitalisation empowers forgotten believers.

5. Revitalisation Values Marginalised Communities

Every year Birmingham City Mission distribute Christmas presents to children who would not be getting them otherwise. There are a number of reasons children get referred to the mission for presents, and there are multiple indices of deprivation at work. According to the mission, in recent years, out of the whole of Birmingham, our postcode has received the most presents. As a church we deliver the majority of those presents, and in the process get to talk with lots of people, and get to tell them about Jesus and about the church. But what kind of church plant reaches this kind of community?

I have heard others say, and am convinced myself, that buildings are important in communities like ours. Being a known presence, a place to come, an open door, is a significant step towards a meaningful relationship. The people in our community are not 'Birmingham' people, they are 'Northfield' people, they are less likely to travel and very firmly rooted in their local context. I remember chatting to one girl who had fallen out with her dad. 'Anyway,' she said, 'I'm never going to see him again, coz he's moved away.' 'Oh right,' I said. 'Where has he moved?' 'Longbridge,' she replied. Longbridge is only one stop beyond us on the train, and five minutes away by car.

There are many in our community who are used to being left

behind. They may have had a whole number of people walk out of their lives over the years. When the guy who ran our Friday night youth clubs moved on, the kids were not just upset, they were *angry*. And the new guy was treated with suspicion for a long time. Short-term, and pop-up style ministries are distrusted. As a result, church in a home, or a school, or a pub, or anywhere else other than a church, is obviously transient and not worth the effort of connecting with in a meaningful way. The local church closing is just another example of a group of people, whom they might have been tempted to trust, giving up and walking away. We need a reality check. Most church planting strategies, as valuable as they are, will simply not reach these people. Bricks and mortar speak of a commitment to still be here in the good times and the bad, the rough and the smooth.

But of course, on estates the buildings are in disrepair, being turned into garages, carpet warehouses, mosques, or like the old Salvation Army hall at the bottom of our road, mixed martial arts gyms. What our estates need are gospel-preaching, servant-hearted, people-filled, bricks-and-mortar churches. Who will be willing to do this work? Who will be willing to give themselves to a life of obscurity and become part of the furniture in a marginalised community for the sake of lost men and women who bear the image of God?

Now, I appreciate that this is the one benefit that is not true of *all* revitalisations, but if we believe in faithful, Spirit-filled, expository ministry, we need to work out how to develop it amongst our poorest people. A church planting model that takes seriously church revitalisation, the kind that intervenes before 'Tiny Steps Nursery' has taken possession of the keys, has the ability to value marginalised communities in a unique and powerful way.

This is gospel logic. It looks small and weak, but it is God using 'the lowly things of this world and the despised things – and the things that are not – to nullify the things that are, so that no one may boast before him' (1 Corinthians 1:28–29). But the inevitable question is, will he do that for us?

6. Revitalisation Uncovers a Hidden Gospel Frontier

In preparing to move to Northfield, I assumed my task was twofold, the internal work of revitalising the church, and the external work of breaking new ground as we reintroduced the community to the gospel. What really surprised me was the hidden fringe of people who were somehow already connected to the church, and who renewed their interest in Jesus as they saw life return to the church. When we had visited and talked with the church we had no idea they were there.

There were people occasionally attending the church who didn't know Jesus. There were family members who had stopped coming to church who began to reconnect again. There were people in the community who had a history with the church. Basically, there was a ready-made mission field of people that the church family already had a love and a burden for but were struggling to reach.

It wasn't difficult to motivate the church to pray for growth, because growth was simply brothers and sisters, mothers and fathers, sons and daughters, friends and neighbours being reached with the good news of Jesus. After about 18 months of hard work both focusing internally on the church, and externally on these people, we began to see fruit. In the two years that then followed we baptised 18 people, and there was probably a 50/50 split between folk who were part of this fringe, and those who had no previous contact with the church.

One local young man had a granddad who attended the church years ago. He was a teenager growing up on the estate. His mum was scared for his future, and told him to read his Bible and sort out his life. He read the Gospel of Matthew, gave his life to Jesus, and turned up to his granddad's church. He was one of the first people we had the privilege of baptising. He and I read the Bible together every week, and he runs the projector on Sunday mornings. Revitalisation uncovers a hidden gospel frontier.

Untapped Opportunity?

Hear me rightly. Church revitalisation is not *better* than other forms of church planting. There are a number of models of planting that have tremendous strengths that are unique to them. The point I am making is that revitalisation is no different. Our problem is that so often we have overlooked revitalisation because we have only ever seen its weaknesses and difficulties.

But wouldn't it be short-sighted to overlook a route towards establishing a vibrant gospel witness, in a gospel priority area, that builds positively on the past and straddles the generations? One that brings spiritual renewal to dormant disciples, may be uniquely placed to reach some of our hardest communities, uncovers ripe gospel frontiers, and through it all necessarily drives us to deny ourselves and follow Jesus in the way of the cross? This is the untapped opportunity of revitalisation. Why would we waste it?

CHAPTER 4:

FILLING THE TANK

'The proposal that Jesus was bodily raised from the dead possesses unrivalled power to explain the historical data at the heart of early Christianity.'[1]

Our church had given themselves two years until closure, and was simply working out how to die well. The question for us was, were any other options *possible?* The answer was, 'Not necessarily'.

In the early nineties I had a T-shirt designed by the West Midlands rock group 'The Wonder Stuff.' On it was written, 'On the eighth day God created Stourbridge.' The joke works perfectly because it identifies the band's hometown, nestled between Kidderminster and Dudley, as the apex of God's creation. I knew it was a joke even back then, because I was from Scarborough, the true pinnacle of God's cosmic purposes.

It is easy to think that our particular little expression of God's worldwide community carries this kind of status. 'On the eighth day God created Crossway Church!' However, we gain a right confidence by losing confidence in ourselves. We must acknowledge who we are, and who God is. Every good thing we enjoy, and every plan we make that comes to fruition is a generous gift of God towards us. Remember King Nebuchadnezzar, standing on the roof of his palace in Babylon, marvelling at his own glory? That very moment he is reduced to eating grass. (Dan. 4) James warns us,

> *Now listen, you who say, 'Today or tomorrow we will go to this or that city, spend a year there, carry on business and make money.' Why, you do not even know what will happen tomorrow. What is your life? You are a mist that appears for a little while and then vanishes.*
>
> James 4:13–14

James is reminding us that just because we have a past does not mean we have a future. In the same way, just because a church has a past, does not mean it has a future. Only God can bring about revitalisation, and he is under no obligation to revitalise *my* church. The picture we briefly sketched in the introduction does not emerge by accident, and not only will some churches die, but some really should die.

As Joshua approached Jericho he asked the commander of the LORD's army, "'Are you for us or for our enemies?' 'Neither,' he replied, 'but as commander of the army of the LORD I have now come'" (Josh. 5:13–14). It is easy to think that God must be on our side as a small struggling church, seeking to be faithful. In fact, some churches respond to their slow demise by developing something of a siege mentality, arguing that the fact that they are shrinking is a sure sign that they must be faithful, and God must be on their side. But to ask whether God is on our side is the wrong question. We need to ask, are we on his side? Being on God's side means being willing to follow him wherever he leads us. It means a readiness to die to oneself for the sake of Christ and his church. This is the heart of discipleship. The LORD is in command, not I.

Before arriving at Crossway I was nervous. At theological college God had shown me I was a people pleaser. The book *When People Are Big and God is Small* was basically written for me.[2] I was concerned that I wouldn't know how to handle conflict, and how to lead the church through the necessary change without disruption. I shared the concern with a more experienced church leader. He explained that the conflicts that change produces are not something to fear, but unavoidable, and wonderfully, actual opportunities for discipleship. No wonder he was always looking for a fight. But, the truth is, our Christian growth is made of these moments; when worlds are rocked, comforts are challenged, and we must decide who is in command.

Of course, just because *my* church may die does not mean his church, *the* church, is dying. 'On this rock I *will* build my church,' says Jesus (Mt. 16:18, emphasis mine). His church is being built, but it is *his* church, not mine. In practice that means some churches will die, some churches will be planted, and by God's grace some dying churches will be revitalised. As has been noted, 'Jesus loves his church. He loves not just healthy, growing churches, but he also loves sick, struggling churches. Jesus loves churches that need revitalisation, and we should love what Jesus loves.'[3]

In church planting circles, we readily acknowledge that some churches die and some are planted, but we don't often acknowledge that some churches should be revitalised. In this chapter I want to suggest three theological foundations that 'fill the tank', and give us the confidence to consider revitalisation. As we gain confidence in God, false confidence in ourselves, our churches, and our favoured methodologies will begin to melt away, and we will be fuelled to pursue the task before us with joy.

1. God Gives Life

Jesus said to a festering corpse, 'Lazarus, come out!' (Jn. 11:43). The explanation of the empty tomb of Jesus was 'He has risen!' (Mk. 16:6). 'The universe was formed at God's command, so that what is seen was not made out of what was visible' (Heb. 11:3). And the same God 'who said, "Let light shine out of darkness,"' makes 'his light shine in our hearts to give us the light of the knowledge of God's glory displayed in the face of Christ' (2 Cor. 4:6).

If, as we saw, one of the arguments against revitalisation is that 'it is easier to give birth than raise the dead', the obvious reply is, *'For whom?'* Our God loves to breathe life into dead things, loves to make something from nothing, and loves to choose the 'things that are not' to nullify the things that are. Our God loves revival, and he loves revitalisation. His acts of recreation and resurrection bring him glory!

It might have been possible, under God, to establish a new church plant in Northfield. But as I think about the context, it would have been a real tragedy if we had allowed fear to stop us considering revitalisation. According to the Church Urban Fund website our parish is in the top 8% most deprived parishes in the country. There is a history of faltering church plants locally, as they have struggled to stay the course and make inroads into the community. Because of an arson attack, the Anglican church was burnt down 15 years ago, and it was the only other church building on the estate.

Buildings matter in communities like this. History matters. Because God loves revitalisation we now have a multi-generational church family, meeting in the heart of the large housing estate, with a building that gives us an accessible, well-established and visible presence in our mission field.

God was gracious in bringing about the right personal circumstances for it to happen. He was gracious in initiating the right conversations. He was gracious in the gathering of a core team. He was gracious in the existing church responding so positively. He has been gracious with every subtraction and addition. He has been gracious with every conversion.

But in the first instance, God was gracious in revitalising our hearts, as a church family. It is hugely challenging that Paul describes our faith, the faith we share with Abraham, as faith in 'the God who gives life to the dead and calls into being things that were not' (Rom. 4:17). Abraham's body was as good as dead, and Sarah's womb is more like a tomb, and yet they remained fully persuaded that God had the power to bring forth new life. Paul then helps us to see that our faith is no different. Our faith is in the God 'who raised Jesus our Lord from the dead' (Rom. 4:24). Why believe revitalisation is possible? Because, as Peter says as a matter of fact, 'God has raised this Jesus to life, and we are all witnesses of it' (Acts 2:32).

Fundamentally, God has been gracious in revitalising our church because God has been gracious leading us back to his enlivening Son. As with all gospel ministry, revitalisation demonstrably requires the miraculous recreational power of Jesus Christ from day one.

2. God Gives Gifts

We must remember that *'God has placed the parts in the body, every one of them, just as he wanted them to be'* (1 Cor. 12:18). It is easy to look at a particular context and immediately formulate a 'wish list' of the kind of people you think it will take to get the job done. However, revitalisation means by its very nature that God has not finished with the people he has there. There is nothing wrong with praying for a new guitarist, as long as with equal fervency we are thankful for the organist celebrating their 70th year of service. We must not overlook what God has already given us in the people who make up the body.

Early on at Crossway Church, I worked closely with two key people. The first had been an elder in the church for well over 30 years, and had been key in us being able to begin the revitalisation. The second was a Birmingham City Mission outreach worker who had been based at the church for several years. We were praying and serving well together, and the existence of these two godly men and their families had really convinced my wife and I that coming to Northfield was the right thing for us.

About four months in, the first had to step back from all activity for health reasons and the second broke the news to us that Birmingham City Mission were ready to move him on to a new context.

It floored me. I didn't know how I would be able to continue without them and felt like giving up.

However, because that happened, God opened my eyes to the gifts he had given to other people, and he continued to give us all that we needed in a remarkable way. What we think we need and what we actually need are often two very different things. I experienced something of a mini 'Gideon moment'. For Gideon 32,000 men were whittled down to only 300, in order to ensure that God alone was the one glorified in victory.

When we dictate what we think we need for ministry, we are also presupposing the kind of opportunities that will come our way. What was so amazing to me was the way that God gave us opportunities in ways that were perfectly tailored to the people we had available as a small fellowship. Early on a young couple came to us with significant marital difficulties. If we had been a fledgling church plant we would have really struggled to support them practically, but having older 'grandparent' figures meant there were people on hand who were willing to offer hospitality, counsel, and show the kind of love that helped them navigate a very difficult season. Our stay and play group is hosted by a number of mums who, though exhausted, are doing an incredible job of befriending other local parents. However, it is also hosted by a number of grandmas. With no children in tow, they have time to draw alongside anyone in need, love nothing more than to talk parenting, will gently introduce them to Jesus, and carry a genuine love that drives them to prayer. One of our church members is a former alcoholic, who at this late stage of life has such a clarity on the gospel of grace and the faithfulness of the Lord Jesus, and can speak so frankly and simply, that he has become something of a 'secret weapon' amongst our discipleship of addicts. I could give further examples, but you get the point!

3. God Gives Growth

The final thing to remember is this word from Paul. 'I planted the seed, Apollos watered it, but God had been making it grow. So neither the one who plants nor the one who waters is anything, but only God, who makes things grow' (1 Cor. 3:6–7).

Behind the first two points is the simple conviction that God works by his Spirit through his word to bring about new life and equip us for ministry. How does God give life? He speaks. How does God prepare his people for works of service? Through the ministry of his word.

We can't plant and water any old thing. We must plant and water the seed of the gospel. A farmer may rightly be pleased with a harvest, and credit his hard work for the crop. But, lest pride should creep in, it is also worth pointing out that he had to use a particular seed. He would not have got the same yield from pebbles or jellybeans.

God's prophetic word of judgement and salvation brings change and bears fruit. 'You have been born again, not of perishable seed, but of imperishable, through the living and enduring word of God' (1 Pet. 1:23).

Ultimately only one thing is necessary for change, growth, and fruitfulness: the activity of the Spirit of God, through the application of the word of God. It might be tempting to think that because God is the one who makes things grow, we therefore do not do anything. But actually, it is clear that our task is to plant and to water. We have a responsibility to actively and deliberately fight for the gospel to take centre stage in all we do.

In Isaiah 55, God is also the one who waters.

> *As the rain and the snow come down from heaven, and do not return to it without watering the earth and making it bud and flourish, so that it yields seed for the sower and bread for the eater, so is my word that goes out from my mouth: it will not return to me empty, but will accomplish what I desire and achieve the purpose for which I sent it.*
>
> Isaiah 55:10–11

There really is no stopping God's word.

Growing up in Scarborough, my childhood often consisted of trips to the arcades on the seafront. A classic within the seaside amusements *oeuvre* was 'whack-a-mole'. It was a table made up of holes, and each time a mole appeared out of one of the holes you had to hit it as hard as you could with a mallet. It was a game of tantalising skill and strategy. Whatever you did, the pesky mole would always reappear. He was relentless, tenacious and indestructible. If you read through the book of Acts it becomes clear that we have in our hands the 'whack-a-mole word of God'. Nothing can stop it. However hard it is hit, it continues. David Peterson describes the word of God as the 'the real hero of the Acts of the Apostles'.[4] We simply need to let the hero speak.

When we arrived at Crossway Church there were so many 'things' that needed to change, but the first thing we needed to do was rediscover our confidence in the gospel, and God's powerful activity through his word. Fruitfulness was not going to be brought about through painting, planning, programming or publicity, but through preaching and teaching. If we were willing to give God the room to speak, he would lead us into the necessary change required. Were we willing? What did that mean?

Our first conversations together were going to be key, and that is the subject for the next chapter.

Is this God our God?

Before we go there, although it may be stating the obvious, these three theological truths, that God gives life, God gives gifts, and God gives growth, all presuppose that God, in his nature, delights to give us good things. Jesus encourages us to ask, seek and knock. He says,

> *Which of you, if your son asks for bread, will give him a stone? Or if he asks for a fish, will give him a snake? If you, then, though you are evil, know how to give good gifts to your children, how much more will your Father in heaven give good gifts to those who ask him!*
>
> Matthew 7:9–11

But do we ask? Are we praying, regularly, fervently, persistently, for God to act in this way?

If we are not praying in this way, expecting him to act, then why is that? It is right to lose confidence in ourselves, but we must never lose confidence in him. When we forget that God is gracious, the first danger is that thankfulness becomes entitlement, so we think that God *must* revitalise our church because we have been faithful for so many years. The second danger is that faith becomes fear, so that God *could never* revitalise our church, because perhaps we were responsible for killing it in the first place. Both dangers have lost sight of the character of our God who delights to give undeserved gifts to his children.

CHAPTER 5:

RELEASING THE BRAKES

'How many free-church leaders does it take to change a light bulb?'

'Change? What do you mean, change?'

Take the B1447 right to the end and you will arrive at Robin Hood's Bay. It is a traditional fishing village, in breath-taking surroundings, clinging precariously to the cliff face. At first glance, it looks like it could be washed away with the next high tide. Further down the coast huge chunks of boulder clay are bitten off each year, and the paths need to be continually rerouted. In fact, along the Holderness coastline the present coast is around 4km inland from where it was in Roman times! However, unlike the surrounding terrain, the geology upon which the village was built is not soft clay deposited in the last ice age, but tough beds of calcareous siltstone dating back to the middle Jurassic. Robin Hood's Bay is going nowhere.

Church can feel vulnerable: a small community, clinging on for dear life, and susceptible to being carried away by the next spring tide. However, the Bible assures us that God has provided us with solid bedrock upon which to build. Whatever the surrounding geology, whatever the forecast, we have a firm foundation. At Crossway Church, as we began to talk together about revitalisation, we had to stop worrying about the clay, identify again the solid ground and sift carefully through the landslips and fossils for what would be kept, and what would be left to the encroaching sea.

It is easy to think that what revitalisation needs is simply 'change'. The church is dying, so everything must go! It is right to have an expectation of change, and 'change' was on the agenda from day one. However, it was not simply change for the sake of it. I am not sure we got everything right, but we made each change with a conviction that it was necessary.

As uncomfortable as it may be, beginning down the road of revitalisation means at least attempting to answer the question of what has happened to bring about the decline. We must ask, 'What has gone wrong?' But self-diagnosis is a dangerous game. Depending on temperament it can work both ways: some of us may pop to the GP to get something for that persistent headache only to discover it is much more serious. Others may be in the process of getting our affairs in order and saying our final goodbyes, when the mortality rate connected with housemaid's knee is actually very low.

But, in a sense, that illustrates precisely why grappling with some kind of diagnosis is important. Often our instincts are incorrect, and our subsequent prescriptions are misplaced and ineffective. Not that long ago I was in a room with a number of leadership teams of struggling churches. Around my table I could sense the burden they carried for their churches, the loss of confidence in the gospel, the fatigue and helplessness. Meanwhile the talk at the front involved unveiling the latest silver bullet: 'café church'. As effective a strategy as that may have been for the church leader speaking, to simply prescribe a solution in this way made huge assumptions about the churches in the room, and about what had really gone wrong. The result was an audible, exhausted sigh, from pretty much every person sat around my table.

But churches do not die without reason, and there are some very helpful resources available to help us to diagnose well.[1] I want to simply outline some of the key questions we asked ourselves at the beginning of the process to help us identify the kind of change that was required, and which I pray are useful for those facing a similar challenge.

1. Are We Leading Through the Bible?

I don't think any church would want to admit that they have consciously decided to stop being led by the Bible. Most of us belong to churches that claim Scripture should take centre stage in all we do. However, over time, seemingly small decisions can end up creating a culture where there is very little room to allow God to speak, on his own terms, through his word.

The leadership team may be selected, not with an emphasis on their ability to teach God's word, but on their ability to manage the day-to-day administration of the church. This may then lead to a reliance on occasional, visiting preachers, week after week. Expository ministry quickly become an atomised string of stimulating lectures around popular passages of Scripture.

Sermons stop being 'challenging' and instead become 'interesting'. A Bible study group may become a context that emphasises the ingenuity of the expositor – drawing out smart devotional insights, like a rabbit from a hat – rather than a context for humble submission to the plain reading of the text.

Where this is the case, the good news of Jesus can very quickly become assumed rather than actively and deliberately taught and applied. After all, everyone has known each other for years anyway. It would be a bit embarrassing to go back to basics and actually ask 'what is the gospel', wouldn't it?

It was very revealing when we sought to adopt a clear statement that articulated the central tenets of the faith. This pattern of ministry had led to confusing and contradictory convictions about the gospel itself, without them ever being challenged and corrected. If the church does not know the biblical gospel, then what hope is there for anyone else getting to know it? Because of this, revitalisation must begin with reformation.

2. Are We Connected to the Community?

A pastor I spoke to recently, who had led his church through a revitalisation, put it this way: 'The narrative of the community had changed, but the narrative of the church had stayed the same.' There had been an effective season in the past, in which the church had listened carefully to the community it was reaching, and contextualised appropriately. However, the community had now moved on, and the church stubbornly continued its traditions, becoming less effective with each year that passed.

Of course, the gospel itself does not change, but the language in which it is spoken rightly changes depending on the hearer. As has often been said, 'We change the method not the message.' Our Bibles were not originally written in English, but their translation is a key step of contextualisation that is necessary for effective communication to take place (at least for most of us). For many churches there are equivalent steps of translation that are simply not happening with the ministry they are engaged in, because they are steps that were not required in the past. When I arrived at Crossway Church, not only was much of the ministry of the church incomprehensible to the non-Christian community around us, much of it was incomprehensible to other Christians as well. For example, on a Sunday morning the family service followed a 'breaking of bread' service, with a coffee break in between. If you came early to the flagship Sunday service we were hoping to grow, you would walk into a meeting of silent reflection, without explanation, in which you might well be expected to make a contribution. Not only could the church feel unwelcoming, it felt impenetrable.

The church may be culturally disconnected from the community, but it may also be geographically disconnected. For many members their only relationship with the community they are seeking to reach is driving in for a church service on a Sunday morning. We may feel we are geographically close because the building is there, but the church is the people, not the building. Bricks are important, but they cannot love people or tell people about Jesus. Some of us are a lot less geographically rooted than others. If you are a busy professional you may live and work in different cities, and then socialise in another location again. To then simply add a fourth postcode to the satnav for church seems normal. But many other people think parochially, perhaps because the circumstances of their lives mean they are far less mobile, and if they are ever going to be reached with the gospel, then geography matters, and taking a more rooted approach is required. If the vast majority of the church family live outside of 'the parish' that will have a huge impact on your ministry.

3. Are We Organised for Evangelism and Discipleship?

There may well be a lot of activity in the church, but are these contexts in which the good news of Jesus is being carefully explained in an understandable way? Often a church will seek to reverse decline by launching a new 'outreach' event, like a youth club, with the hope that this will somehow turn around the church.

If a youth group is being launched, it is important to ask what the pathway is for a young person to hear about Jesus, begin to follow Jesus, join the church family, and grow in the context of community. It may all be hypothetical at this stage, but still something to be prepared for. It is also important to recognise that this will not happen by Christmas, or even in the first few years. If you launch a club, are you prepared for that to be at least a ten-year commitment before you even begin to reassess its viability? Do you have a plan for Mum or Dad? Does your strategy begin with a youth club, but go on to engage with the whole household? In theory at least, how will it do that?

In the end of course, any activity can be a total red herring. Evangelism happens as we talk to people about Jesus. In order to do that we need to have confidence in the gospel itself, and to be equipped to know how to communicate the truth of the gospel to others. It does not require youth clubs, café church or messy church, and it does not require new initiatives. More often than not all it requires is *time* and *boldness*, two things that the UK church has in short supply.

It is worth reflecting on whether or not the church is organised well enough for conversion growth. How will someone hear about Jesus, respond to Jesus and begin to learn how to live with Jesus as Lord?

4. Are We Expecting Growth or Decline?

Part of the problem is that we do not really believe that God will do it, and that begins to show in the way that we make decisions. Choices are made on the basis of what will work well for the existing church family, what will be most convenient, what will fit into our busy lives. Decisions are driven by the need for greater comfort, rather than the need of the Great Commission.

It is not that any rash changes have ruined things in a single afternoon, but hundreds of small decisions to play it safe, and prioritise those on the inside over those on the outside, have resulted in a structure that is no longer fit for purpose. Small decisions have a big impact, and failure to be ready for growth will guarantee the ongoing trajectory of decline.

We can tell ourselves that they really are very small things, that it wasn't that long ago when the work was flourishing, and that if it were necessary we could always change things back. One of the effects of nostalgia is that it makes the passage of time feel much shorter than it has actually been. Quite frequently I would ask roughly when the story that had just been told had happened, or how long ago it was when they saw these kinds of things going on in the church. The figures I was told must, logically, have been wrong. 'Recent' baptisms were actually ten years ago. Work that had 'only just been completed' on the building was actually 20 years ago. The days when the balcony was regularly overflowing with youth were easily 40 years ago.

5. Are We Really Willing to Change?

The author James Bartholomew popularised the term 'virtue-signalling'.[2] It gets to the heart of a common tendency we have to align ourselves with a particular cause without it ever having to cost us anything. Social media is rife with 'virtue-signalling'. We change our profile, or re-tweet a cause, letting everyone know our morality by conforming to a particular hashtag, but our lives display little evidence that the issue is as close to our heart as we make out. As Bartholomew notes, 'Saying the right things violently on Twitter is much easier than real kindness.'

Well, guess what: talking energetically about change is much easier than changing. Reading a book on revitalisation is much easier than releasing the brakes and beginning the process. There is a real danger in the church of virtue signalling by attending the right conferences, learning the right language, and even deciding on the right change, without it ever turning into action. Billy Bragg once sang, 'The revolution is just a T-shirt away!'[3] For us, it might be tempting to sing 'The revitalisation is just a members' meeting away'. The truth is implementing real lasting change is going to be much harder than that. How, then, can we bring it about?

CASE STUDIES 2 & 3:

REVITALISATION AND CLOSURE

TIM SUNDERLAND, GOODWAY ROAD

Goodway Road was a small church on a housing estate in the north of Birmingham. They had started as a Brethren Assembly and over time had affiliated to the Evangelical Fellowship of Congregational Churches (EFCC) and the Fellowship of Independent Evangelical Churches (FIEC). They had seen a steady decline in numbers over several years. The church consisted of an elder and his wife, two housebound ladies and a very active older lady. There was also another couple on the fringe of the church. They had no engagement with the local community at all, and were dependent upon other churches for support, including the provision of a preacher each week.

In 2007 they approached our church for help with the preaching, and sensing something of an opportunity, my family and I were sent to work for the church with the hope that we could help to lead something of a revitalisation process, or if not, to help it to close. After discussions with the church elder, EFCC leaders and the FIEC church restoration leader, where we discussed the challenges and changes ahead, we began working with the church in the summer of 2007.

Our aim was that with the support of other local churches and Christians we might be able to restore this gospel work and its witness.

We did a number of key things:

- We tidied the building in order to make it useable. With the support of other Christians, we threw out a lot of things that had been accumulated in unused rooms and decorated where necessary.
- We gave the church a new logo and sought to make the community aware of our presence and our new activities.
- I met with other local church leaders and made them aware of what we were trying to do and sought their support with the hope that they might have people who wanted to join our work. During this time, I met a young Christian family who lived in the community and were looking for a new church. They decided to join with us and threw themselves into the work.
- We leafleted the local community and invited them to a holiday club at the end of August, run with the help of young people from our sending church. We used that to launch a weekly children's club. Some of the numbers were encouraging and we made fresh contact with a good few families in the community.

- In the September my wife, with an elderly lady at church and another young mum started 'Jelly Babies', a baby/toddler group. Again, the number of those attending was encouraging.
- The church service was moved from a Sunday morning to 4pm on the afternoon and we sought to make it more accessible to the community with refreshments and children's activities.
- I sought to build some links with local primary schools and discussed how I/we might be able to support the RE curriculum. I was able to get a Canadian Christian drama group into the high school to take an assembly and some lessons.
- Our Christmas event was a high point, when the children's club put on a modern-day nativity and the building was full of families from the local community.

However, by Easter 2008 we were pretty sure the work would not be able to continue. In the end, the church had waited too long to seek help. Their numbers had reduced dramatically, the elder was tired of holding it together and there was very little energy or enthusiasm to start a new work. There was a lack of willingness and commitment from some within the church to make the changes necessary, despite these being highlighted in early discussions. We were also unable to find enough significant support from other local churches/Christians. It would have taken much more than simply a new family or two, and a burst of activity, to truly bring about revitalisation.

PHIL WALTER, FIEC CHURCH REVITALISATION COORDINATOR

As Revitalisation Coordinator for the FIEC, I have learned very quickly that some churches, for many and varied reasons, will have to go through the painful process of dying. However, a church can die well and impact the spread of the gospel, or it can pass away with sorrow, regret and perceived failure.

Come with me to a village in Bedfordshire, the home of a once thriving village work, blessed by God and in its heyday seeing folk saved, baptised and discipled. As time has elapsed, the church has become geographically isolated with few houses in the direct vicinity, and as a result has had to face up to a dwindling congregation, which stood at just seven elderly but passionate believers. What are they to do?

This dilemma faces numerous churches in the UK as they confront this reality. There are many aspects that need to be considered. The experience of this church was painful, long and far from easy. What will happen to the members? Will they be cared for? What should we do with the building? How do we distribute any funds we have left? When do we stop meeting? How are we going to tell the community? What are the legal requirements? These questions and many more were earnestly prayed about as they sought after God's will in this. FIEC Practical Services were on hand to assist in the areas requiring specialist knowledge but the church battled with 'How can we die well?' All of which can seem huge mountains to climb. However, as we shall see, facing up to such reality can bring great potential for gospel growth.

What has happened is for me a template of what a church can do to still be involved in the Great Commission.

First, they emptied their bank balances! They distributed their not insubstantial finances among the missions they supported. This was a great blessing and contributed much to the sense of gratitude to God that they felt as they were able to give in a positive manner.

Second, they decided on their last Sunday Thanksgiving Service to remind all who came of the years of God's blessing upon the work. God in his goodness raised up this work many years before, and it was helpful to them to finish with a recognition that this was about Jesus and his church.

Third, they put the building up for sale, which subsequently was purchased by a developer. Was that the end? Certainly not! The money from the sale has been given to a church plant through the FIEC. The group have sought to stay together as they joined another church, and now meet up regularly to pray for the church plant they have funded. This links them positively with the gospel work that their decision to die well has funded. They have become partners in the gospel.

It is sad to see a church close whatever the circumstances, but this church died well and left a legacy of new life in a wonderfully fruitful way.

CHAPTER 6:

GETTING IN GEAR

'We put up with anything rather than hinder the gospel of Christ.'[1]

Change is hard. For most people change is hard. It is not only traditional churches that are 'set in their ways'. A hip and trendy church plant that seeks to modify things six months in will also experience resistance. Resistance to change is not a symptom of old age. I was amused when my eight-year-old daughter told me she would still be calling Crossway Church by its old name because she didn't like change.

I once heard Ray Evans, the senior pastor of Grace Community Church in Bedford, explain that change is difficult because it involves loss. When we lose something we grieve for it, and grief is made up of two primary emotions: sorrow and anger. It is a helpful reminder to me that when a change is introduced, something is being taken away. If people are upset or angry it is probably not because they hate me, or because they are working for the enemy, but because they are Christian believers dealing with the emotions that have arisen from their loss.

Although grief cannot be avoided, there are ways to mitigate its effect. The key one to mention here is *the communication of a clear vision*. I suspect a key reason changes fail to hold, or manage to do disproportionate damage, is because of a communication problem. If a vision is clearly communicated, then it becomes clear why a particular change is a priority issue, and it manages expectations of what the outcome will be. Someone may struggle, for very understandable reasons, to accept a particular change, but may still be able to understand the logic behind it and actually share the same vision of what the church is seeking to be and do.

Another reason communication of a clear vision is important is that it forces me to carefully articulate *for myself* why a change is necessary. Change, because 'other churches do it differently', or because 'I prefer things done differently', or because 'well, we need to do something differently', are arguments that rightly sound hollow, and expose my own motives. Once a change is made, there is always a tendency for it to revert back to the way it was, and I am then required to spend energy defending the decision. If I cannot articulate a sound reason for the change, then I am not yet ready to make it.

The rest of this chapter will outline four key questions that needed answers in order to facilitate healthy, vision-led change at Crossway, and they are questions that need to be answered in any church aiming for revitalisation. As we talked together we were very consciously trying to cut through the clay back to the rock. There were an infinite number of changes that could have been made, and an infinite number of ways for me to spend my time: kitchens, car parks, kids' clubs, men's breakfasts, café church, messy church, guest services, gospel services, breaking of bread services, pet services (OK, there was no pressure for pet services, but I just wanted to check you were still reading).

We asked ourselves four important questions: What is it that has brought us together? What are we aiming to do together? Where does our authority come from? How will we make decisions together? Once we established answers to those questions, the necessary changes became obvious as well as possible.

1. What Has Brought Us Together?

A church is not a club formed by a committee, it is a community formed by Christ. At Pentecost Peter tells us that it is Jesus, at the right hand of God the Father, in heaven, who has poured out the Holy Spirit on his people, and given them his power (Acts 2:33). Throughout the book of Acts, the true hero, the word of God, is the apostolic witness to the resurrected Jesus. In Acts chapter 20, as Paul addresses the Ephesian elders he describes the church as being of God, bought with his own blood (Acts 20:28). There is nothing natural about this family. It is wrought entirely through the supernatural work *of* God, at the command of Jesus, by his Spirit and the word of his gospel.

Our normal instinct when we are threatened is to go into self-preservation mode. The minute people begin to talk about change, our defences go up, and we begin the process of damage limitation. However, we are not self-created, so we cannot be self-preserved. The thing that has brought us together is not simply a shared tradition, but a shared Saviour, and he is unchanging. As together we cling to the one who does not change like shifting shadows (Jas. 1:17), we are free to allow necessary change to take place.

It is easy to postpone change because of a fear of conflict. We think that because the church is united in Christ, we must demonstrate that unity by avoiding conflict at all costs. However, it is Christ who gave us unity, and it is he who will preserve that unity. We did not establish our unity, and we cannot preserve it through our own personal management of the status quo.

Paul's prayer at the end of Romans is insightful:

> *May the God who gives endurance and encouragement give you the same attitude of mind toward each other that Christ Jesus had, so that with one mind and one voice you may glorify the God and Father of our Lord Jesus Christ.*
>
> Romans 15:5–6

Unity is a gift from God, and as Paul prays for it, he also prays for endurance. Endurance is needed because on the ground, in the context of community, it will remain hard work. I am not advocating arbitrary conflict, but if Christ has brought us together, and community requires endurance, then the goal is surely not no conflict, but healthy conflict. For many church families, conflict means church splits, bitterness, and anger. But, as we answer the question of what brought us together, as we become clear on the gospel, and the source of our unity, we begin to create a context for healthy conflict to take place; conflict with patience, forgiveness, forbearance, faith, hope and love.

2. What Are We Aiming to Do Together?

We often assume we share the same vision of what it means for us to meet together as a church family. The reality, however, is very often our expectations of the gathered church are quite different. For some the focus is almost entirely upward: church is about a personal engagement with God. For others the focus is almost entirely inward: church is about the sweetness of Christian fellowship and practical service. For others still the focus is almost entirely outward: church is only really church if it is on mission.

We spent time looking together at God's design for healthy local churches. As a leadership team we read and discussed 'Deliberate Church',[2] not because it contained all the answers, but as a tool to identifying what assumptions we had, and where any disagreements or misunderstandings lay. I preached a series from Ephesians at the church, even before we came, before they had made the decision for the revitalisation to go ahead. We spent much of the first few months in Bible study, reading articles, and dreaming big dreams together. We told stories of the past, encouragements and discouragements, we identified the big and small ways God was at work right now, and we began to consider why we do things the way we do them.

It became clear that there was a real disconnection between the vision and what actually happened week by week. One particular word that came up time and time again was *accessibility*. Much in the church was inaccessible to anyone who was not already part of the furniture. I don't mean physically inaccessible. There is a beautiful ramp to the front door of our building. But, it was impossible to imagine a route a non-Christian could take from the point of first contact to converted, active, church member. In short, unless you were already a committed Christian who understood a very particular model of worship, it was an uncomfortable experience.

In one sense the question we were grappling with was, *'Who is all this for?'* Is it for the sake of those who are already in the church, or for the sake of our local community? Would the community even notice if Crossway Church had died? It brought us back to some key dilemmas: are we about ministry or maintenance, commission or comfort, people or programmes? The necessary changes became obvious. Some were apparently big: service times needed to change, particular meetings needed to close, new groups needed to launch. Some were apparently small: the language we used, the songs we sung, the notice boards and brown curtains. But every change could be articulated in terms of the vision of who we were seeking to be, and the mission of who we were seeking to reach.

It was costly, it stretched our relationships, and required a lot of prayer. It looked foolish at times, especially when in the first year no one really joined the church beyond that core team, we saw no one converted, but instead conducted five funerals. Without the communication of a clear vision we would have quickly lost heart and lost our way, but God has sustained us, through success and failure, sound steps and foolish mistakes, and we are just beginning to see the vision become, in part, a reality.

3. Where Does Our Authority Come From?

It should come as no surprise that it is Jesus who is in charge of his church. The leaders of a local church do not have an inherent authority of their own. As a pastor, any authority I exercise is mine only through the word of God. It is true of course that I may well have been granted a delegated authority through a process of selection, recognition or ordination, but the reality is that I have authority to the degree with which I am in line with the authoritative voice of Jesus in the Bible.

If Jesus is ultimately leading the church, then as a local church leader, as I seek to envision the congregation, it is not my voice that matters. It is his. My first priority is to make sure Jesus has room to speak through his word.

By way of example, before the revitalisation process began, the church had been entirely reliant on visiting preachers. In fact, it was expected that elders would ordinarily not preach in their own church. As a result, there was a disconnection between God's word and the church's community life. That means a disconnection with decision-making, discipleship, mission, discipline… pretty much everything.

A change we discussed was a move to majority in-house preaching, which was made possible because there would be a full-time pastor committed to a ministry of the word for the congregation to which he belonged. We spoke about what that would look like: me, preaching at least three out of four Sundays, from day one. We also talked about a long-term commitment to prayerfully raising up future elders who would be willing to minister God's word within the church family.

Such a change involved very real loss. There were many good friends and 'old favourites', regular fixtures in the church calendar, who would no longer be invited to preach, simply because there was not the space. Not only that, but instead they would have to listen to me every week, a younger, far less experienced preacher than many of those they were used to.

The priority to give Jesus the room to speak through his Word wasn't just about Sunday morning preaching. It also played out in the way we changed the other meetings, the way we formulated a strategy for outreach, and the way we are seeking to build an infrastructure for healthy discipleship.

4. How Will We Make Decisions Together?

Key to us remaining united as we began was gaining clarity on how to make decisions well. With the arrival of a small core team there could have easily been a 'them and us' mentality. Also, with the prospect of a considerable agenda of change, there could have easily been a sense of it being imposed upon the congregation from above rather than it being agreed upon together.

However, when we arrived there was ambiguity around who the members of the church were, how leaders were appointed and how the decision-making process worked. That was clear in the lead-up to us coming, and meant there was some confusion and misunderstanding that needed to be worked through in the first few months.

The MP Tony Benn famously said, 'Holding the powerful to account involves asking five questions: What power have you got? Where did you get it from? In whose interests do you exercise it? To whom are you accountable? And how can we get rid of you?'[13] Unless you can answer those questions clearly, it is very difficult for trust to develop, for unity to flourish, for decisions to be made, and for real, long-term change to take place. It became an important priority for us to establish a meaningful membership and eldership, and a process for appointing both.

This involved us preaching through a statement of faith and adopting it together, introducing a constitution and governing document, formally recognising the membership of the church and appointing an eldership. For a new church plant, this is the kind of work that is done behind the scenes, long before the church is launched. For us, it had to be implemented alongside normal church life.

This may seem like overkill for a small church. However, if the decision-making process is entirely informal and relational, it only takes one person to disagree before it becomes personal. Having a clear, even-handed process through which change is implemented deliberately depersonalises the decision, allowing for everyone's voice without singling out an individual, or allowing them to disrupt the process.

It is not an act of faithfulness to pander to every whim, or try to keep everyone happy. In fact, faithfulness requires that we resist what is sometimes described as the 'tyranny of the minority'. One of the reasons decay sets in is because there is effectively a hostage situation, a vocal few who are somehow able to dictate all decisions.

I remember a conversation in which we were seeking to make a decision and someone responded, 'There are some who will not like this.' I asked who those people might be; especially given most of the active church family were present in the room. The suggested protesters were two people who were permanently housebound and would therefore be unaffected by the change, and a third who had actually passed away six months earlier. It is not kind or loving to allow a congregation to be held hostage in that way. Introducing a clear membership and decision-making process were key to us implementing change faithfully.

Unhindered Ministry

To be honest, it was hard work. Any dream of a 'honeymoon period' was shattered from day one. It meant conflict. It involved many long conversations with a few unhappy people. Understandably there was some suspicion; there was some misunderstanding; and sadly some people left. But by prioritising the clarification of these aspects of our church life, the result is that five years down the line, we are enjoying a season of great unity, with a high degree of trust. The whole membership has a voice, and there is an unambiguous process by which change can be decided upon and implemented. It was amazing to see just how far God had brought us when our recent decision to change the name of the church took only two discussions and a single vote.

With each of these four questions, we were forcing ourselves to make decisions for the sake of people we had not even met yet, people on the outside of the church, and getting ourselves fit for purpose and ready for growth.

CHAPTER 7:

SETTING OFF

'God is always doing 10,000 things in your life, and you may be aware of three of them.'[1]

In a former life I was a singer-songwriter, a wandering troubadour, peddling songs of unrequited love to any who would listen. Not many did, but it did get me out of the house. I have played such prestigious venues as the local scout hut and the 'Dog and Duck'. My worst ever gig was the BRMB (now Birmingham Free Radio) Christmas party. With the promise of 'good exposure' I was invited to serenade a bar full of DJs and media execs, who were, let's say, 'letting down their hair'. What they needed was Abba's *Greatest Hits* on repeat. What they got was me. It was so bad that at one point I snapped a guitar string and not a single person noticed.

Because of the noise, it was very hard to know what was going on, and how it really sounded. It felt frustrating and pointless. I staggered to the end of my set, and the next band went on. Escaping the revelry, I headed to the toilets downstairs, only to discover that although you could hardly hear anything in the bar itself, the PA was being piped into the toilet speakers beautifully. The band sounded great. On the surface it was chaos, but underneath there was clarity, precision, and sweet music. I wondered who had paid a visit during my set.

The last five years of revitalisation have looked pretty chaotic on the surface. It has been very difficult to measure viability, progress and success. It has been hard to know what has been going on, and if you were to visit us today, you might well say that is ongoing. There are times when it feels frustrating and pointless. However, if you were to see underneath, it is amazing how God is working with clarity and precision. He is producing sweet music in our midst. But expectations are key when we set off, and that is the focus of this chapter. At Crossway, four particular expectations have been hugely important for us:

1. Expect it to Be Long Term

It was 12 months before we saw any real encouragements, and 18 months before the dust really began to settle. I can distinctly remember our second Christmas being a massive encouragement to the whole church, and there being a new sense of being a family with a shared vision and mission. It was two years before we had our first baptisms, and it has only been the last couple of years that we have seen Christians who have moved into the area consider us a viable church to join.

There was much internal work to be done, and much to get us ready, before it actually began to bear fruit. God was doing all kinds of things and I was aware of about three of them. Early on, my brother said to me, 'Don't overestimate what can be done in one year, and don't underestimate what can be done in five.' I have returned to that wisdom often.

I suspect it is not just the experience of a church revitalisation. Any new attempts to engage a local community take time to bear fruit. It takes time to understand the people we are seeking to reach and to speak the gospel intelligibly into their lives. It has been important to slog it out, remember why we are doing what we are doing, and trust there is sweet music somewhere amid the chaos.

2. Expect it to Be Low Key

I have no silver bullets. We are not impressive. Our public profile is miniscule. If you visited, you would probably wonder if you had stepped back in time to the 1950s. We are working on some of that, but we have found that although growth through church transfer might require a slick, attractive operation, if your goal is growth through conversion, there are more important things to give your time to.

We did have a few Christians with itchy feet come and check us out when they heard 'something was happening' at the church. They didn't stay long, when they realised just how much hard work it was being part of our church. At the time I was gutted, but looking back I am really thankful that we did not have too much mission drift. I should have been more willing to gladly embrace obscurity if it meant we had fewer distractions and more time to focus on lost people.

In terms of outreach, I think for some folk in the church, revitalisation was misunderstood as a return to the heyday of the Billy Graham crusades – and with it a return to the activities, programmes and emphases they used to enjoy. We have committed ourselves to a continual refrain of 'people not programmes' and have sought to develop only as much organisation and structure as has been needed to get us to the next stage in our relationships with people in our community.

Investing in relationships is much harder work than launching programmes, but whenever we begin a new initiative we try to make sure the flourishing of meaningful friendships, where the gospel can take root, is our highest priority. In a way it is helpful when things are low key, because all you have left to offer people is Jesus.

3. Expect it to Be Hard

Church revitalisation is not a benign activity. Satan hates any endeavour that has the making of new disciples as its goal, and his opposition can take many forms. Opposition can come from within the core team, from within the existing congregation, from sending churches, from other local churches who may not understand what you are doing, from para-church organisations, from disaffected Christians living locally, and from secular organisations unhappy that a sleepy, dormant congregation is beginning to show signs of life.

According to Ephesians 6:12, however, 'our struggle is not against flesh and blood, but against the rulers, against the authorities, against the powers of this dark world and against the spiritual forces of evil in the heavenly realms'. It is easy to make flesh and blood people into our enemies, when in fact they are people who need to encounter God's grace, just like us. We must remember that the enemy is Satan, and stand firm by taking up the shield of faith, with which we can extinguish 'all the flaming arrows of the evil one' (Eph. 6:16). James writes that God 'gives us more grace. That is why Scripture says: "God opposes the proud but shows favour to the humble." Submit yourselves, then, to God. Resist the devil, and he will flee from you' (Jas. 4:6–7).

As we retain a posture of submission to God, as we live in reliance on his ongoing provision of grace, we are to take our stand against the devil's schemes. Slow, tenacious perseverance is the order of the day for anyone involved in the task of revitalisation. I have committed myself to a deliberate daily 'plod for God'. It does not look exciting or attractive, but I believe it is what is required of gospel ministers seeking to faithfully lead a church through this kind of change.

4. Expect to Grow

When we get used to decline, it soon becomes all we can imagine. Pretty soon a 'culture of can't' develops. Of course when you aim at nothing, you hit it every time. If we set our expectations too high we can quickly become disappointed, frustrated and cynical, but if we set them too low, we will not be ready for the growth God may choose to give us.

It is worth asking, 'If God answered our prayers, would we be ready?' We might instinctively say 'bring it on', but without thinking through the implications of our outreach strategy actually working! This is especially important when it comes to the discipleship of new believers. We found that we quickly reached capacity, were caught on the back foot, and as a result didn't support and pastor people as well as we should have.

There is a false assumption that 'people not programmes' means being disorganised. Actually, one of the key ways we are trying to become better ready for growth is by getting as organised as possible. I have been challenged to 'skill up' so that there is spare capacity, and we are operating slightly ahead of our own curve. We have consistently found that God gives you what you are ready for. The challenge is for us to own a big vision together and be ready for it to become a reality.

A small church that begins to grow will encounter significant challenges. What works organisationally with 25 people will not work with 50 people, and what works with 50 will not work with 100.

Sometimes we have a perception that small is beautiful. Church can be highly relational, so that everyone knows one another, and communication is straightforward. Church can be simple, so that there is little need for complex structures or programmes. A visitor is identified within seconds, invitations are spontaneous and leadership structures are flat and operate on the basis of consensus. Church can be immediate, so that a newcomer can quickly enter community life and understand its culture. There is easy access to the leadership team who are available for any and every occasion and need. Church can be united, so that decision-making can be highly democratic with everyone basically on board with the direction of travel. Church can also be active, with little room for coasting. Everyone is recruited, involved and with a clear job to do.

In the early stages of a church revitalisation, though these qualities are not automatic, they may be fostered relatively quickly as you reform as a church family. That can be hugely encouraging for a church that has been struggling, and that is enjoying the sweetness of close community again, perhaps for the first time in years.

But if a church begins to grow, those qualities become increasingly difficult to hold on to, and a church doesn't have to get very big before small stops being beautiful. Tim Keller has said that 'once [a church] gets to 40+ people, the intense face-to-face relationships become impossible to maintain'.[2] Ray Evans suggests the figure is lower even than that. He notes, 'A church that ... grows from twenty to around fifty has already lost some of the greatest benefits of small-group intimacy.'[3]

What this means is that, from the moment you begin the process of revitalisation, you will be saying goodbye to the things that made you an attractive community to be a part of. It may be that some of the cultural aspects associated with small church will need to be actively *resisted* in order for others to be truly welcomed into the church. It may be that the church views itself as highly relational, but has in actual fact outgrown its ability to do that in an organic way, and as a result is becoming cliquey and stand-offish.

We found that though early on we could provide the support, accountability and biblical input that was required to nurture new disciples in an intuitive and informal way, we have quickly had to address the issue of how we do that well now that God has given us modest growth. We are seeking to disciple new believers in three key contexts: the large group Sunday morning context of God's people assembled together to hear the word preached; the small community group context of God's people meeting in homes to study the word together, and prayerfully support each other; and the one-to-one context of two believers meeting to apply God's word deeply and with accountability. Helping people to access those three contexts does not happen by accident, and we are having to think through how we organise and train ourselves well to continue to make these pathways of discipleship effective.

Of course it all still looks very chaotic on the surface, though hopefully not as anarchic as the BRMB Christmas party. We do not have all of the answers, and we are trying to learn from as many others as possible. But expectations are key, and I am convinced that if we commit ourselves to thinking long-term and low key, expecting it to be hard work, and yet remain ready for growth, then quietly, in the mess, slowly but surely, God will make sweet music.

CASE STUDY 4:

REVITALISATION AND GOSPEL PARTNERSHIP

DUNCAN WOODS, TRINITY CHURCH SUNDERLAND

Duncan Woods was an assistant minister at Christ Church Durham until 2010, and during that time developed an awareness of the gospel need in the north-east of England. During his time at theological college, he and his wife, Laura, prayerfully considered a return to the north-east, and a potential revitalisation opportunity arose.

Sunderland Free Church recognised they were struggling. The church could no longer afford to employ their pastor, and had been praying for external help from other churches for some time. Through their connection with the North East Gospel Partnership two other churches heard their cry for help, and began to consider a revitalisation project. Partnership between gospel churches on the ground has been key to developing this work. Christ Church Durham had a gospel concern for Sunderland, and they provided people. Christ Church Newcastle helped to provide on-the-ground support and mentoring. Partnership led to the revitalisation, and the revitalisation has led to greater partnership as these NEGP churches work and serve together.

After a period of preparation, including much talk of change and the existing pastor moving on, a team of 21, including Duncan and Laura, came and joined the church, which was then relaunched in September 2013.

The original church itself had been planted around 1980, and had dwindled in number from nearly 100 down to ten over the next 30 years. Although there was an evident love for others, there was a temptation to circle the wagons in the face of a changing and hostile world. When all you have known is decline, it is easy to lose confidence in the gospel. Slowly but surely secondary, often cultural, issues become primary.

As the work of revitalisation began, the power of the gospel and the unity of God's people were two key priorities. On arrival, Duncan preached through Ephesians, being clear on the gospel, and precisely where our unity comes from.

The eight remaining, mostly elderly, members of the congregation could easily have felt outnumbered and powerless, but it was important to make it clear that they were loved and would not be treated in a deliberately insensitive way. Instead of immediately launching small groups, they spent time meeting together as a single group, thinking through what it meant to be a gospel church, a community church and a local church.

That paved the way for their third key priority, mission. In the church there were different expectations of what that meant, but it has been wonderful to see particular people personally revitalised in their mission and ministry zeal.

The church has seen modest numerical growth, in a place where people rarely move into the city. As a result, it takes time to make meaningful connections with local people. In these early stages there has been growth, partly through a few reconnecting with church, but mostly through internal spiritual renewal, transfer from other churches to support the work, and Christians who have moved into the area for work.

Over the last few years there have been some gracious encouragements. It has been wonderful to see faith in the power of the gospel grow again. It has also been encouraging seeing older folk overwhelmed by how loving and attentive many of the younger core group are with them. There have been good examples of people who have been disconnected from church, now part of a vibrant word ministry again, but it is slow. There have been two years of slow graft, meeting one-to-one with one particular individual. There have been two and a half years developing a meaningful relationship with someone at the school gate, who is now open to meeting and reading the Bible with Duncan's wife, Laura. As a couple they have committed themselves to a long-term and low-key work here, with the great prayer being one of indigenous conversions amongst members of the local community. As we chatted, Duncan reflected on the fact that revitalisation does not sound very captivating. It doesn't have the same appeal as church planting. It can feel very weak and fragile. But they are willing to give themselves to a 30-year ministry here, if God will so have it.

Revitalisation has many strengths. Duncan can see that there is an immediate credibility with the locality because they have moved in to support a local church community. It is also not threatening to other local churches as revitalisation doesn't rub people up the wrong way in the way that church planting sometimes can. The pre-existing church family have been invaluable in helping to understand the city, how people think, and the history of the community. They have also helped challenge preconceived missional ideas that the core team may have come with.

It is also hard work. It is hard not knowing what changes may trigger upset and conflict. Changing the way the Lord's Supper was conducted and introducing the use of a projector have been less of an issue than anticipated, but apparently small things like removing old, stored, ministry cassettes and hymn books was a much greater concern. The question of how much change should be begun and when is an ongoing issue. Duncan has probably been more cautious and restrained than others might be, and at times wonders if he has not been assertive enough. The wisdom of knowing when to push for change and when to hold off and be sensitive is required constantly.

As Duncan reflects on all that has happened, he is clear that it has been worth the effort. The model of revitalisation has given them a foot in the door of the city that it would have been foolish not to take advantage of, with many practical benefits. But it is also evident that he believes in the theological importance of revitalisation. This is the same gospel, for a different era, and we don't always need something 'new'. Having to work with others, particularly older believers, is a sign of a healthy church in the New Testament, and helps to guard against the arrogance of youth.

We must rejoice in the church planting of recent years, but

there are examples of it being done by a younger and often restless generation (in which Duncan includes himself). Working with older believers connects us with our heritage and reminds us we are not the first to discover and pass on the gospel. The church should be multi-generational, and multi-cultural. Start-ups can carry an inherent danger of homogeneity, uniformity and sometimes arrogance towards other gospel initiatives. We must not dismiss previous generations. We need our older brethren to teach us. They have experienced so much more of life, seeing God's faithfulness through many seasons. It is a joy to see older Christians counsel younger Christians on parenting, work, life priorities – to simply 'gospel' them. It is tempting to ride roughshod over our history, but God is in the business of revitalisation. He believes in it and so should we.

CHAPTER 8:

ALONG THE WAY

'It is about a road which begins many miles before I could come on its traces and ends miles beyond where I had to stop.'[1]

If we have attended all of the conferences, and we have read all the books, and we know how to be fluent in the language of [insert favourite ministry stable here], it is very easy to lead with all the phrases and gestures.

Rather than leading from a deep conviction about the nature of God, his gospel, and his church, we instead develop a portfolio of poses depending on the context in which we find ourselves.

Of course there is much to learn from others, and we must never let our personal convictions about ministry stop us from listening carefully to others and allowing them to correct our blind spots. However, many local churches have suffered terribly at the hands of leaders whose perpetually shifting emphases mean that they never work out who they really are.

I hope that, as we have proceeded, much that we have grappled with resonates with your own deeply held, biblically informed, convictions about healthy church ministry. However, in this chapter I want to briefly outline three healthy postures for revitalisation that have sustained us through the last five years. These are not mere gestures to be employed from time to time. Unless they become permanent postures for ministry they will not support us along the way.

1. Be Faithful with Those God Gives You

In chapter four we talked briefly about the way that God gives gifts, and that he has 'placed the parts in the body, every one of them, just as he wanted them to be'. However, it is one thing to acknowledge someone's value. It is another to care for them well.

Tim Keller has said, 'While in a larger church, the people will let you pastor them if you are a good preacher, in a smaller church people will listen to your sermons if you are a good pastor.'[2] There is a renowned talk from the Evangelical Ministry Assembly in 1986 in which Phillip Jensen is heard to urge ministers to stop visiting the sick because it is taking them away from gospel ministry.[3] I suspect he is deliberately overstating his point to make it: we are ministers of the word, and we will fail in that task if we do not say 'no' to some of the demands placed upon us. We must actively fight against simply becoming chaplains for Christians. However, it is very tempting to take him literally, and in doing so excuse a straightforward neglect of the flock. Taking on revitalisation means taking on a congregation in which sick people must be visited, families mourned with, and funerals taken. If Keller is right, this is crucial if the church is to let you lead through the word.

In our context, there was one older lady who was the wife of a former elder in the church. I never had the privilege of meeting her husband, but his godly reputation and influence in the church was very evident. His wife was a remarkable woman, who had been at the centre of the church community for many decades. She was increasingly housebound, and I took it upon myself to visit her from time to time. I didn't do it perfectly, but periodically I would clear a couple of hours to make the trip, read God's word, and pray with her. She took an interest in the changes to the church, despite finding them difficult to hear at times. She grilled me about decisions we had made, wanting the logic behind it all, before then always seeking to encourage me. Strikingly, though she was no longer physically present in the church week by week, she still had a huge influence amongst some of the other older members, and it mattered to them greatly that I had visited her. It changed the way they viewed me. It changed the way they heard me. It also had a positive impact on the way they approached the changes that were being made. Her biggest concern was whether or not I owned a suit to wear when taking her funeral, and when that time eventually came, I made sure I dressed appropriately!

But Jensen is partly right. We must preach well if we are to lead well. We must give our very best to that task. And we must know how to say 'no' to anything that will take us away from that. It is easy to feel stretched and overwhelmed, and so it is vital that we are realistic and honest about what we can take on. How many sermons can we prepare for in a consistent and sustainable way? Is there is an expectation that you will preach twice on a Sunday and once midweek? Will you really be able to do that and invest enough energy in the process of change and reaching the lost? And will you really be able to feed the sheep well each time?

Paul urges the Ephesian elders, 'Be shepherds of the church of God, which he bought with his own blood' (Acts 20:28). The members of our churches were purchased at the highest price. And as his under-shepherds, he has entrusted them into our care. I wonder if we truly know the value of those we are called to serve? We must be faithful with those God has given us.

2. Be Focused with Your Strategy

John Benton has said, 'Churches never become great by being self-pitying and ingrown. They become great as they nurture a genuine love for the glory of God and for the souls of lost men and women.'[4] It is easy to wallow in self-pity. There are Christians living locally who have chosen not to join us; deal with it! There are other thriving churches in neighbouring areas; they are under no obligation to send me their people. We can feel pressured to adopt a strategy that simply mimics what others are doing. Instead, it is our responsibility to nurture our love of Jesus and our lost community. Focus on that.

Making mission a priority means it will come at the expense of other things. It may mean dearly loved activities have to stop. It may mean dearly loved people choose to leave. For a small church, losing members often seems the single most important thing to avoid. But if not losing members is the number one priority, mission won't be.

In a larger, stronger church, if the pastor says 'no' to something good, it may simply mean equipping a team to do it instead. When things are fragile and small, if the pastor says 'no' it may well mean the whole church has to say no. Be patient, stay focused, and choose one or two core ministries to do well.

This is actually an extension of our care for the flock. If you are small in number, then everyone feels a pressure to be a part of everything for it to be viable. It is important to be careful how much you ask of people. Too much, too soon, spreading people too thinly is a recipe for burnout. It is also self-defeating. No one is ready to give a reason for the hope that they have, because no one has time, and everyone is exhausted.

It is easy to think that in order for new life to enter the church then more stuff needs to happen. In actual fact it may well be that so many activities are running that it is stopping people from giving quality time and effort to core tasks of evangelism and discipleship. A church must act its size. If you are a few in number, then revitalisation may actually require you doing much less rather than much more. It can be incredibly draining to belong to a church that is struggling to grow and that is consistently attempting to act significantly bigger than it is.

Being small can also result in a kind of heavy shepherding that comes about almost by accident. Leaders know everyone so well, know what everyone is doing with their time, and is friends with most of the church on Facebook. It is easy to become overly involved, controlling and directive in terms of pastoral care and serving in the life of the church.

Keep it simple. By doing too much, everything is done badly. By doing the key things well, mission remains central, people remain passionate, and the church begins to bear fruit.

3. Be Thankful in Everything

Sometimes we can be so enamoured with the vision of where we would like to be, we fail to see how much we have to be thankful for right now. Be thankful for who you are as a church today. Be thankful for what God is doing in you. Be thankful for the people God has given you. Be thankful for another day to gather together under his word. Be thankful for *everything*, and celebrate together the wins, however small they may be.

We have deliberately made a habit of identifying the evidences of God's grace in each other's lives and our labours. We have found it an incredible tonic against fatigue and disillusionment. In our first year, as part of our prayer meeting, we committed to pray for a new 'friend of the church' each month for a year. Amazingly, every time we gathered we could look back and identify the individual we had befriended, spurring us on to pray more boldly.

We run Christianity Explored almost continually, but we run it in very small groups, and ordinarily as a one-to-one with a person or couple who are interested in the gospel. It would be easy to become frustrated by the fact that we don't have large seeker courses that draw big numbers, but that is simply the stage we are at, and it is a truly wonderful thing that there seems to always be someone that God has given us at that stage.

In fact, there are many positives to running seeker groups as one-to-one's. People are increasingly suspicious of large, anonymous courses, the discipleship can continue after the official course has ended, there is a freedom to get quickly to the heart of the issue, and a deep friendship develops from pretty much week one. What could be a cause of frustration is actually yet another reason for thanksgiving.

We have committed ourselves to a ministry of thankfulness with the ones and the twos that God has given us. We must never slip into comparison games with other churches, which will only rob us of our joy in the Lord. As we pray for fruit, and see that come in the form of small but significant encouragements, we can celebrate together the wins, in a way that testifies to the power and love of God.

Confident Clarity

Faithfulness, focus and thanksgiving: three postures to sustain us in the task of revitalisation, through a process that will be long-term and low-key, and yet keep us striving for growth.

These postures are helpful because they give us clarity on what to do when we don't really know what to do. Henard speaks of effective church revitalisation probably taking at the minimum seven to ten years.[5] It is not always obvious what the strategy should look like throughout that process. It is important that we don't become impatient, trying to run before we can walk. We must learn what it means to wait well for real lasting change to come, and to remain confident in the simple ministry we are engaged in along the way. If we are faithful with those God has given us, we will preach with care and commitment, and we will pastor people in a way that allows the refining fire of God: the breaking and remoulding that needs to happen in God's timing. If we are focused with our strategy we will give time to personal evangelism, thinking in terms of people not programmes. If we are thankful in everything, we will give ourselves to prayer, recognising that only God can revitalise his church.

CHAPTER 9:

POTHOLES

'What is our hope, our joy, or the crown in which we will glory in the presence of our Lord Jesus when he comes? Is it not you? Indeed, you are our glory and joy.'[1]

It would be easy to think of the church revitalisation journey as a steady march towards ecclesiastical peace. It would be easy to tell stories and present case studies with a whiff of triumphalism and self-improvement. In reality, it is a journey entirely dependent on the grace of God, a journey of perseverance, and tenacious endurance. It will also be a journey that understands that true peace is not achieved on earth, but received from Jesus, and is found in eternity. We are not building heaven here.

When Paul and Barnabas return to Antioch after their first missionary journey they visited the churches they had previous planted in Lystra, Iconium and Antioch. It is the only insight the book of Acts gives us into the content that early Christian believers were taught by the apostles. The verses simply state:

'They returned to Lystra, Iconium and Antioch, strengthening the disciples and encouraging them to remain true to the faith. "We must go through many hardships to enter the kingdom of God," they said' (Acts 14:21–22). The first priority for the new believers was that they would be given a right expectation for the journey ahead, and that journey would be full of many kinds of hardships.

The experience of church revitalisation will vary from case to case, but the requirement for endurance is universal. In this chapter I want to draw out a few key potholes we must successfully navigate and overcome through perseverence.

1. The Potholes of a Church Revitalisation

Revitalisation often begins with a small church. We have already identified some of the potential blessings of small church. Small church can be beautiful, but its limitations are always clear.

First, there may be a *limited leadership*. The idiosyncrasies of one or two individuals may well have been allowed an unhelpful amount of airtime. If a church has been struggling for a while, then immature and outspoken believers may have been granted significant control over ministry areas. If the church has been managing decline, with few new leaders, individuals who have stayed the course may strongly believe they are entitled to set the direction simply by virtue of length of service.

Idiosyncratic individuals given free rein will result in idiosyncratic practices in church life. When, for a long time, it has been 'us four and no more', traditions that alienate outsiders are left entirely unchallenged. It might be the way singing is led, welcomes are given, birthdays recognised, notices announced. It might be to do with the furniture and fake flowers, curtains and coffeepots, biscuits and books. It would be easy to say none of this matters, but the reality is that each idiosyncrasy is an unnecessary barrier to people encountering God through his word. We all have them, whoever we are, but wherever they can be identified they should be addressed.

I remember in a preaching class at college having my own idiosyncrasies pointed out to me. The sermon had been passable, but I was told to go away and watch myself on video to observe the visual barriers I was putting in the way of people engaging with God's word. I wasn't pulling disco shapes or making obscene gestures, but the way I carried myself physically was clearly upsetting our tutor. It was hard for me to take, and uncomfortable for me to watch, as well as being incredibly helpful feedback to learn from.

As we encounter idiosyncrasies in this way there are a number of important points to remember. Please pick your battles carefully. Not everything needs to be addressed immediately, and it may be too much to handle if it does.

It is tempting to go for the easiest things first, or the most prominent things, or even the things that most annoy you, but think about an order of priority, so that the things that most directly affect gospel ministry are the first things addressed. As you do that, expect conflict. As we have mentioned before, conflict is not something to be avoided. There will certainly be conflict when cherished idiosyncrasies are challenged. For that reason, it is hugely important not to make it personal. Make sure in your own heart that this is not about your personal preference or hobby horse, or simply a personality clash. And through it all, seek to be humble. Invite scrutiny and feedback for all of the changes that you are seeking to implement.

Secondly, there may be *limited resources*. This may again relate to people. There may be a struggle to find within the church family people who are able to serve in key areas of the life of the church. Very often the struggle is with kids' work and music, two of the most prominent aspects of church life. It may relate more to the finances of the church, or the limitations of the building. As a church family you may be firmly resolved to be unashamed of the gospel, and yet find yourselves seriously ashamed of the toilets.

A key resource limitation is time. Early on, everyone will be involved in everything. You will be a church of generalists, who roll up your sleeves and put your backs into whatever is required. There is the same number of needs in a small church as there is in a large church. The only difference is the number of people who have that need, and the number of people who are able to meet it. As a result there is a tension. There will be a strong pressure to begin to get specific, you may even have someone with the right gifts, but no time to specialise effectively.

These are not bad things to be avoided, but good things to work towards in the future, as you take the long view. The danger is that, as you enter the situation, rather than spending your time cultivating a faithful gospel ministry, you become overwhelmed by the limited resources, and give your time to filling the gaps in the rotas yourself, perpetually fundraising, improving the fabric of the building, or launching ministries for every presenting need.

Patience is essential. Trust in a God who equips us with all that we need to do the ministry he calls us to, today. Patience requires us to act our size. The shape ministry takes will reflect the limitations of your resources, and although it will be tempting to try and mimic what other churches do, you only need resources, human, financial, or otherwise, to support the ministry today. Tomorrow can look after itself.

However, whilst you seek to be patient, cultivate a godly discontent that works towards something better. Primarily that will mean investing in the people you have, training them as well as you can, for the next stage.

Thirdly, there may be *limited vision*. It has been said that, 'When you are winning nothing hurts, but when things are hard, everything hurts.' The inherited situation is likely to be one in which the church has felt vulnerable for a long time. Beyond the gospel itself, victories may feel like distant memories. When was the last baptism? When was the last time a visitor came two weeks' running? When a family joins the church it feels like revival, but when a family leaves, it is devastation. The default vision of the church, though it doesn't appear on the official website, is (to borrow from Gloria Gaynor), 'we will survive'. It may even be phrased as an uncertain question, 'Will we survive?'

Devoid of any clear vision beyond survival, and with an ongoing resignation to the status quo, the result is not *no* vision, but *many* visions. Each member present will have their own idea of what needs to happen, and of what the future should look like, and as has been often noted, diversity of vision spells division. It is hard to move beyond maintenance mode. At least survival is something we can all agree on.

Alternatively, it may also be a vision that is looking not to the future but instead to the past. As we have noted, nostalgia breeds inertia, and we can be so enamoured with former success and prominence, that we are blind to the present need. In this kind of institutionalised pride the church, on the brink of closure, looks at the chaos and sees only its pedigree and provenance. Pride gives birth to complacency, when it should provoke collective repentance and faith.

The answer is to shepherd the church. The shepherd feeds his lambs, supplying for them what they need, within the love of Christ (Jn. 21:15). Not by being domineering, but by being examples to the flock (1 Pet. 5:3). And, it is as we commit ourselves to God and the word of his grace, that we are built up and given an inheritance amongst the sanctified (Acts 20:32).

As we let God speak through his word, so he will begin to replace faltering sight with a compelling *vision of God*. We will be drawn to repentance as we grasp his holiness, we will be encouraged to pray as we grasp his goodness, we will step out in faith as we grasp his glory, we will be filled with joy as we grasp his grace.

He will begin to revitalise our diverse agendas with a united *vision of the gospel*. We will see our shared depravity and condemnation, shared Saviour and salvation, shared grace and new identity. There is neither them nor us, neither old nor young, neither dying church nor core team, for we are all one in Christ Jesus (Gal. 3:28).

He will begin to enable us to resist resignation to 'what is', in favour of a desire for 'what could be', through a faithful *vision of the church*. We will rejoice in the eternal, central, glorious design of God's new community. We will recognise the evidences of God's grace that permeate all that we do. We will be thankful for his provision, whatever that may look like. We will trust that God knows what he is doing and delights to use weak people to fulfil his Great Commission.

He will begin to turn us from a myopic nostalgia, to a confident *vision of the future*. Self-preservation will become self-sacrifice, as we look to a hope beyond this world. Maintenance will become mission, as we lay up our treasure in heaven. Evading risk will become enduring anything, as we live for a hope and a joy in eternity: a glorious crown made up of men and women, young and old, from all walks of life, who have turned to Jesus – in part because we chose to say 'yes' to revitalisation.

2. The Pitfalls of a Church Revitaliser

Whatever our good intentions, whatever our skill or gifting, our biggest pitfall is us. Our sin can have a devastating impact, with toxic fallout, destroying any good we have done. The fruit of such a ministry will be harmful, whatever noble name we give it. Our sin is common to man, but it is also specific to us. There are many things one could highlight at this point, but I want to briefly identity three 'church revitaliser's sins' that I think may be a particular temptation for those of us embarking on such a journey. We need to know ourselves, and our limitations, as we set off.

The first church revitaliser's sin is *pride*. We all struggle with pride, as our sinful nature demands autonomy from God, and we place ourselves at the centre of the world. However, misplaced confidence in ourselves, belief in our own ability, and pleasure in our own achievement can manifest itself in specific ways in the midst of a church revitalisation. Seeking to be God's instrument in bringing life to a church, can very quickly turn into seeking to bring life to that church ourselves – and seeking the glory for our success.

Pride leads to arrogance, and a belief that we hold the answer to any problem. It leads to overwork, and a belief that we must do everything now. It can result in either a controlling dominance, or a crippling fear of man, both driven by an unhealthy obsession with our own reputation. It can make us defensive, anxious, angry, protective, mean, manipulative, selfish, opinionated, outspoken, isolated, and solitary. A forthright and proud leader placed in a vulnerable and fragile context is the perfect trigger for an atomic explosion.

The second sin is *self-pity*. There is unlikely to be a honeymoon period in a church revitalisation, and it is easy to begin to wallow in my own troubles. 'It shouldn't be this hard,' I cry. This can quickly become an ongoing, excessive self-absorption that leaches all joy out of my walk with God, and from my gospel ministry. I struggle to see what God is doing, and feel that he is neglecting me. Self-pity is closely related to pride, because it is so often driven by a feeling that I deserve better. I am a misunderstood, unfortunate and unhappy, victim.

Self-pity leads to a sense of entitlement. It plays comparison games and begins to covet the blessings received by others. It leads to a greedy ambition, not for the glory of God, but for self-validation and self-promotion. It lacks any contentment with the way things are, any thankfulness for the privileges I have, any trust in the sovereign hand of our Lord. It can make me lonely, bitter, resentful, attention-seeking, faithless, prayerless, sarcastic and harsh. It is like a stellar implosion: a black hole sucking us in on ourselves.

The third church revitaliser's sin is *cynicism*. This may be a general hopelessness about the way things are, along with despair about the future. It may also be an increasing irrational distrust of others, their motives, their gifts, and their integrity. Accompanying everything that takes place is an internal jaded monologue, suggesting it is fake and phony. Nothing is going to change. Growth isn't possible. They are lying. This is pointless.

Cynicism leads to a kind of radical scepticism. Instead of carefully questioning a new idea, it interrogates it with the assumption that it will fail. It is pessimistic to the point of paralysis. Cynicism also leads to favouritism, side-lining part of the church in favour of those who fit my demographic. It can make me dismissive, prejudiced, frustrated, sneering, and full of contempt towards others. It is devoid of faith in God, and his activity in our lives. It stops us learning, stops us trying, stops us trusting, and stops us praying.

Thanks be to God, that Jesus has decisively dealt with my grotesque sin in all its forms, through his death on the cross. 'After he had provided purification for sins, he sat down at the right hand of the Majesty in heaven' (Heb. 1:3). It is painful just typing out definitions of these sins, but the guilt has been removed. The blood of Christ cleanses 'our consciences from acts that lead to death, so that we may serve the living God!' (Heb. 9:14). As ashamed as I may be, seeing these many failures, I fix my eyes again on Jesus, 'the pioneer and perfecter of faith. For the joy that was set before him he endured the cross, scorning its shame, and sat down at the right hand of the throne of God' (Heb. 12:2).

He turns my pride into humility. He did not exploit his position, but took on the nature of a servant and humbled himself to the point of death (Phil. 2:6–7). He 'opposes the proud but shows favour to the humble', and he gives us more grace (Jas. 4:6).

He turns my self-pity into self-sacrifice. Though his soul was overwhelmed with sorrow to the point of death, he said, 'Yet not what I will, but what you will' (Mk.14:34–36). He teaches me the secret of being content in any and every situation, knowing that 'I can do all this through him who give me strength' (Phil. 4:12–13).

He turns my cynicism into faith. A woman pours expensive perfume over Jesus' head. The disciples see only waste, but he says, 'She has done a beautiful thing' and immediately connects her act of faith to his death and burial (Mk. 14:6–8). At the apex of the most cynical act in history, Jesus says, 'Father, forgive them, for they do not know what they are doing' (Lk. 23:34). He teaches me that though I hold the treasure of the gospel as a jar of clay, though gospel ministry is an experience of being continually given over to death for Jesus' sake, I do not lose heart.

Potholes, Pitfalls and Perseverance

Don't look in, look up, confident of this, 'that he who began a good work in you will carry it on to completion until the day of Christ Jesus' (Phil. 1:6). We can persevere through potholes and pitfalls, because God perseveres with us.

> *And this is my prayer: that your love may abound more and more in knowledge and depth of insight, so that you may be able to discern what is best and may be pure and blameless for the day of Christ, filled with the fruit of righteousness that comes through Jesus Christ – to the glory and praise of God.*
>
> (Philippians 1:9–11)

CASE STUDY 5:
REVITALISATION AND GOSPEL VISION

STEVE ROBINSON, CORNERSTONE CHURCH LIVERPOOL

The opportunity came about because I was thinking through planting a church in my home city of Liverpool, and was approached by the leaders of Ramilies Road Chapel to talk about what it would look like for me to become their pastor. In light of what the leaders were sharing about the church, the conversation became one about what it could look like for us to replant the church. We used the word replant, to make it clear we meant starting again, with a complete overhaul, and starting with everyone of one mind about the way forward.

We brought together two groups of people: the existing congregation at Ramilies Road, and a team of 15 people from a couple of different churches in Liverpool. I worked with both groups of people separately for a number of months and then brought them together to worship in September 2009. For two months we worshipped and lived as Ramilies Road had done, which gave us the opportunity to get to know each other before we officially began working through the replant process. I and two other guys who came as part of the new team joined the existing eldership, and we formed a new eldership to start the process of change and replanting.

Ramilies Road had been a Brethren church, planted 70 years ago, that had faithfully preached the gospel in the Penny Lane area of Liverpool over many years. The Sunday school had at one time thrived. In the 1960s, if you had arrived in Liverpool to study at the university, Ramilies would have been the church to belong to. However, the congregation was ageing, people were leaving, the culture was changing, the community around them needed to be reached.

For more years than they were comfortable with, they have been burying more than they had been baptising. The remaining leadership, four faithful and dear gospel men, were trying to lead the church and manage the decline, as younger people and families were leaving, and the traditional Brethren brothers and sisters were resistant to change. The task of trying to keep people together without upsetting anybody was proving to be an impossible task, and in fact it was becoming destructive. Even introducing another hymn book was resisted, and the changes they sought to introduce were simply not radical enough. People were becoming frustrated and stopping attending, because nothing was happening, and nothing was changing.

What made the replant possible was a combination of desperation, gospel-heartedness to see people saved and won for Jesus, and a willingness to change without compromising the truth of the gospel. It was important that I had permission and room to lead clearly, and that we did not shy away from conflict. Key to all that we have seen God do, has been the prayerfulness of faithful people, particularly a number of ladies who had prayed for many years for gospel change and who are still a part of Cornerstone Church today.

As we came in, the first priority was leadership. Everything rises and falls on leadership. People had lots of ideas for children's work and boosting the current ministries, but unless work was done amongst the leadership then the replant was never going to get off the ground. We made a number of small practical changes but focused on building gospel-centred community amongst the eldership and their families. We worked through theology, gospel values for the church, and modelled community with them. We spent time in one another's homes and faced the tough questions of why the church had got to the point that it had. These honest gospel conversations in the context of community helped us to build unity as we moved forward. One of the existing elders told me that he had spent more time after the first three months with the other existing elders, in and out of each other's homes, than he had in the past 30 years.

The second priority was to formulate and communicate a big gospel vision for the church and the city. Church planting was on the agenda straight away. That seemed like a pipe dream in the beginning but formed a clear gospel direction and focus for us. In fact, now it is the original folk from Ramilies who bang the church planting drum more than anyone else at Cornerstone.

The third priority was the establishing of gospel-centred, expository, pastoral, preaching. The church had never had this, as it had adopted a pattern of welcoming a visiting preacher every week.

I can speak of many encouragements. Seeing the prayers of people who had struggled for many years being answered, seeing people saved and a church now full of families. The church had not had children in attendance for years. A faithful group would prepare a children's message and class just in case any children arrived, and these people are now part of our Kids' Church ministry, with more kids than they could have imagined.

People who had approached the twilight years of their lives, and thought that their days of gospel influence had come to an end, are seeing more fruit now than they have for years. Two of the original elders are still serving as elders, and the majority of the original Ramilies Road Chapel are still part of the life of the church. By God's grace, we have planted another church in the Merseyside region, and there are others in the pipeline to happen before 2020.

One of the strengths of revitalisation is that it gives a lease of life to those who think they are past it, and humbles those who think they have it all together, usually the new team. It requires the grounding and humility of the one leading the work, and if it is done without being a takeover, it displays a gospel unity, generosity and sacrifice. The work begins with a ready-made diverse community as young and old people work together, and it stops an unbiblical approach (in my opinion) of simply reaching a single demographic of students, young professionals, or hipsters.

We have older people who may need to grow in theology, contextualisation and missional innovation, but who have often walked many miles of sorrow and joy with Jesus, as parents, single people or otherwise, and this is invaluable in discipleship.

The replant also allowed us to continue to put the financial and building resources of the struggling church to good gospel use.

In many ways, the biggest pitfalls we have faced have related to conflict, amongst both the leadership and the members. But God has graciously helped us to form a leadership that is able to address conflict together. The process has convinced me that conflict is unavoidable and necessary, and it has been encouraging to see a leadership grow, and an atmosphere develop where conflict can be worked through effectively rather than resisted.

My conviction is that revitalisation should be a rhythm and process for all churches and ministries, with some churches requiring the kind of replant that we have been a part of. Despite the failings of the churches in Revelation, Jesus still pursued them, reminding them of the gospel in the midst of the warnings, and we should therefore do the same. It is also my conviction that when brothers and sisters are asking for help to reach their neighbourhood, we are called to play our part and help them to explore what can be done. If you still need convincing of why revitalisation is a good idea, come and spend time with us at Cornerstone. We'll show you why.

CONCLUSION:

ARE WE NEARLY THERE YET?

'We have no idea where we are going, and sweeping, confident articles on the future seem to me, intellectually, the most disreputable of all forms of public utterance.'[1]

In order to answer the question 'are we nearly there yet', we need some idea of where 'there' is. It is tempting to see something grow large and think therefore we have arrived. But the goal is not simply numerical growth. It is also tempting to see the ministry we have faithfully allied ourselves to live to see another day, and call that an achievement. But the goal is not simply longevity. The goal is fruitfulness. That fruitfulness will be born out of a right steadfast faithfulness to the gospel, but will also require us to let go of many of the things that we have allied ourselves to in the past. That fruitfulness will result in numerical growth, but will be far more concerned with healthy, long-term, God-glorifying, Christ-exalting discipleship than simply gathering a crowd. Increased size and survival against the odds are not the same as success.

The goal cannot be *perfect* fruitfulness. Otherwise the answer to 'are we nearly there yet' will always be, 'not until glory'. The task of discipleship, of denying ourselves and following Jesus, individually and corporately, does not end this side of eternity. This means that the ongoing process of revitalisation will not end either, whatever our age and stage. However, I think there is a right sense in which 'arrival' is the point at which a real dynamic of gospel renewal has been re-established, through which God is beginning to bear fruit.

In his book Center Church, Tim Keller identifies four key 'means' of gospel renewal: extraordinary prayer, gospel rediscovery, gospel application and gospel innovation.[2] If we return for a moment to the four key questions of chapter six, then if we have recovered the heart of the gospel that has brought us together; if the application of this gospel into our lives and the lives of those we are seeking to reach is now the heart of what we are seeking to do together; if we have deliberately and prayerfully humbled ourselves under that gospel as the true authority amongst us; and have organised ourselves in such a way that we can make decisions that result in innovative ways to proclaim the gospel; then we have created the space required to allow God to begin revitalisation. It is God that gives life, and it is not automatic, but as we begin to see the fruit of that change, we can rightly say we have turned the page positively in the life of the church.

Keller identifies some of the visible signs of such a renewal. First, nominal church members become converted. Then 'sleepy' Christians also begin to receive a new assurance and appreciation for grace. Non-Christians then begin to become converted as they are attracted to this newly revitalised church, and 'the resulting conversions – sound, lasting, and sometimes dramatic – generate significant, sometimes even astounding, church growth'.[3] The outflow of that is a vibrant worship, a greater grasp of biblical truth, and increasingly authentic expressions of Christian community. Humble, assured believers will then grow into confident witnesses, and begin to impact the contexts they live in, resulting in cultural change. At the beginning of a process of revitalisation, a community may not have even noticed if the church had closed its doors, but by the end the tragedy would be felt by many. It is tempting to say that such results only happen during extraordinary periods of revival but, if understood in a long-term and low-key way, these are also the ordinary visible signs of a revitalised church.

The case studies included in this book testify to that being something God has done. Those involved are prayerfully committed to seeing that happen more and more. If I may return to where we began, and the first wedding in our building for many years, then many of the characteristics of gospel renewal are on display.

A young mother was attracted to the church family because of a Bible holiday club run for her kids by a team at the church. Included in the team was at least one nominal member who had been converted, and one sleepy Christian who had undergone something of a personal revitalisation. The young mother and her kids were welcomed and loved by many in the church. Week by week she would sit under the preaching of God's word, encountering the increasingly passionate and God-honouring worship, and the developing Christian community. She came to faith through a Christianity Explored group we ran for her and her friend. She was baptised, and at her baptism, we met her partner. Something very similar happened with him. After his conversion God began to change his, and her, behaviour significantly. He stopped his 20-year drug habit. He became less angry. They began to communicate, trust each other, address debt problems, and the home became more stable. They knew that honouring God rightly in their relationship meant marriage, and the wedding took place just a few weeks ago. The wedding itself was an incredible public declaration of their faith in God, and desire to be faithful to each other, which challenged many of those present.

The husband asked me to run a new Christianity Explored group with one of his old school friends as soon as they got back from honeymoon. This is one small story, but a ministry of these kinds of ones and twos, a 'plod for God' that produces this kind of fruit, is a sign that God is breathing new life into his church.

Are we hungry for God to do that in dying churches? Are we hungry for the glory and honour of Jesus? Do they drive our holiness, our discipleship, our mission? And to what extent do we long for this kind of gospel renewal in our churches? When was the last time we cried out to God, 'are we nearly there yet' as we petitioned him over the re-evangelisation of our nation? Perhaps the time is now.

Amen, come Lord Jesus.

REFERENCES

Chapter 1

1 Chester, Tim and Timmis, Steve, *Everyday Church* (Intervarsity Press, 2011), 111

2 White, James Emery, *The Rise of the Nones* (Baker Books, 2014), 99

3 Tice, Rico, *Honest Evangelism* (The Good Book Company, 2015), 87

4 Mohler Jr., R. Albert, 'Christ Will Build and Rebuild His Church' in Mohler Jr., R. Albert, *A Guide to Church Revitalization* (SBTS Press, 2015), 7

5 Brierley, Peter, *UK Church Statistics 2: 2010–2020* (ADBC Publishers, 2014)

6 Jackson, Bob, *What Makes Churches Grow?* (Church House Publishing, 2015), 70

7 http://bit.ly/249cOSX (spectator.co.uk)

8 For example, and not wanting to single anyone out, the Baptist Union -1%, Grace Baptists -0.8%, Open Brethren -1.3%, EEFC -3.3%, and Elim -10.9%. (Statistics taken from

Brierley, Peter, *UK Church Statistics 2: 2010-2020* [ADBC Publishers, 2014])

9 For example, according to Peter Brierley the FIEC 20 churches, what was New Frontiers 27 churches, Vineyard 11 churches and the EPECW three churches (from Brierley, Peter, *UK Church Statistics 2: 2010-2020* ([ADBC Publishers, 2014]).

10 Statistics provided by FIEC.

11 Mohler Jr., R. Albert A, 'Christ Will Build and Rebuild His Church' in Mohler Jr., R. Albert, *A Guide to Church Revitalization* (SBTS Press, 2015), 11

12 Dever, Mark, 'The Revitalisation of Capitol Hill Baptist Church' in Mohler Jr., R. Albert, *A Guide to Church Revitalization* (SBTS Press, 2015), 66

13 McKinley, Mike, *Church Planting is For: Wimps* (Crossway, 2010)

Chapter 2

1 Spurgeon, C. H., *Lectures to My Students* (Passmore and Alabaster, Paternoster Buildings, 1887), 176

2 http://bit.ly/2dJJvcd (movements.net)

3 Brierley Consultancy, *Notes on Church Planting* (Unpublished, 2015)

4 Bonhoeffer, Dietrich, *Life Together* (SCM Press, 1954), 15

5 Sandbrook, Dominic, *The Great British Dream Factory* (Penguin Random House, 2015), 154

6 Sandbrook, Dominic, *The Great British Dream Factory* (Penguin Random House, 2015), 158

7 Sandbrook, Dominic, *The Great British Dream Factory* (Penguin Random House, 2015), 156

8 Henard, Bill, *Can These Bones Live* (B&H Publishing Group, 2015), 9

Chapter 3

1 Attributed to Sir William Preece, chief engineer of the British Post Office, 1876.

Chapter 4

1 Wright, N. T., *The Resurrection of the Son of God* (SPCK, 2003), 718

2 Welch, Edward T., *When People are Big and God is Small* (P&R 2012)

3 Croft, Brian, and Beougher, Tim, 'A Road Map to Revitalisation' in Mohler Jr., R. Albert, *A Guide to Church Revitalization* (SBTS Press, 2015), 47

4 Peterson, David G., *The Acts of the Apostles* (Apollos, 2009), 33

Chapter 5

1 For example: Rainer, Tom, *Autopsy of a Deceased Church* (B&H Publishing Group, 2014), Henard, Bill, *Can These Bones Live* (B&H Publishing Group, 2015)

2 See http://bit.ly/1NxHTX7 (spectator.co.uk)

3 Bragg, Billy, 'Waiting for the Great Leap Forward' *Workers Playtime* (Go! Discs, 1988)

Chapter 6

1 1 Corinthians 9:12

2 Dever, Mark and Alexander, Paul, *Deliberate Church* (Crossway, 2005)

3 Originally part of his final speech to the House of Commons as MP, but also recorded in Benn, Tony, Letters to My Grandchildren (Hutchinson, 2009), 49

Chapter 7

1 Piper, John, Tweet by Desiring God, 2012

2 From a paper entitled 'Process Managing Church Growth' found here: http://bit.ly/29rxsNB

3 Evans, Ray, *Ready Steady Grow* (Inter-Varsity Press, 2014), 23

Chapter 8

1 Edward Thomas, quoted in Macfarlane, Robert, *The Old Ways* (Penguin Books, 2013), 37

2 From 'Process Managing Church Growth' found here: http://bit.ly/29rxsNB (cpas.org.uk)

3 The talk by Phillip Jensen is entitled 'Changing The Church' and can be found here: http://www.proctrust.org.uk/resources/. It was part of the Evangelical Ministry Assembly in 1986, is well worth listening to, but the comments I am particularly referring to are around 50 minutes in.

4 Benton, John, *Why Join a Small Church?* (Christian Focus, 2008), 45

5 Henard, Bill, *Can These Bones Live* (B&H Publishing Group, 2015), 110

Chapter 9

1 1 Thessalonians 2:19–20

Conclusion: Are We Nearly There Yet?

1 Clark, Kenneth, *Civilisation: A Personal View* (John Murray, 2005), 227

2 Keller, Timothy, *Center Church* (Zondervan, 2012), 73–76

3 Keller, Timothy, *Center Church* (Zondervan, 2012), 80

CHURCH
REVITALISATION
ALONG
THE WAY
OF THE
CROSS
RENEWAL
JOHN JAMES
FOREWORD BY STEVE TIMMIS